Training
for
Transformation

A Handbook for Community Workers

BOOK 3

Anne Hope

and

Sally Timmel

Illustrated by Chris Hodzi

C Mambo Press

MAMBO PRESS
Gweru, P.O. Box 779
Harare, P.O. Box 66002, Kopje
Gokomere, P. Bag 9213, Masvingo

TRAINING FOR TRANSFORMATION: A Handbook for Community Workers
BOOK 3

Cover design by Chris Hodzi

First published 1984
Reprinted 1985

ISBN 0 86922 261 9

Printed and published in Zimbabwe
by Mambo Press, Gweru
1985

Training for Transformation

Book 3

Preface

All the theories, codes, and exercises in this book have been used effectively with groups in Africa over the past twelve years. However, there is no short cut to effective leadership of groups.

Sensitivity to the needs of the group and quick sure judgments on what will be most helpful at any particular moment, can only be developed through constant practice, complete openness to feedback from participants, critical reflection, analysis, and years of experience.

This book has been reproduced in three parts mainly because it will be easier to use like this in the field than one large and bulky book. Each part belongs with the other two parts.

Part one is basically the theory of Paulo Freire on developing critical awareness and how to put this theory into practice.

Part two is focused on the skills necessary for participatory education. To break the 'culture of silence', people need to gain a sense of self-confidence and know that what they think is important. Therefore methods to involve the group actively are critical in group leadership, as are ways of clarifying and implementing the goals of the group.

Part three deals with the social analysis necessary to develop critical awareness and long-term planning and with the steps needed for building solidarity in people's movements.

This book is written mainly for practitioners. It is a book on how to put basic theory into practice. It is also written to provide educators and community workers with some tools to help people to shape their own lives.

> "Reflection without action is mere verbalism.
> Action without reflection is pure activism."

This book tries to combine both reflection and action in a clear and simple way. The following is a summary of the content of each chapter. A detailed table of contents of each book is found at the beginning of that book.

TABLE OF CONTENTS

Book 1

Book 2

Book 3

Book 3: Table of Contents

Chapter 9

Tools of Analysis

This chapter includes:

1

Chapter 9

Tools of Analysis

"If any man is rich
but shuts his eyes
to one who stands in need,
the love of
God is missing from his heart."
(1 John)

"If any man is rich
and does give help to one
who stands in need,
he only gives the poor man
what was already his.
The earth was made for all,
not just for the rich."
Populorum Progressio
Pope Paul, VI

A.   Why the Poor Remain Poor*

Everywhere the evidence accumulates:
        The Rich are getting Richer,
        and the Poor are getting Poorer.
This is happening not just in one country, but all over the world. We need to analyse and find out why this is happening.

Is there something basically wrong with our system? For years most middle class people believed that people were gradually getting better off. Many thought that if countries could just increase the Gross National Product, all would be well. Everybody recognised that there were a few serious problems, but some people had confidence that these could be solved, through making the existing system function better.

---

* From a working paper of Father Frank Vanderhoff, St. Paul's University, Ottawa, Canada, doing field work in Mexico, 1973.

Functional Change

Society includes a number of institutions, held together by values and ways of doing things that have become accepted. Some groups have become marginal, squashed out of the circle of well-being, and some sociologists saw the task as finding ways to include these again, to provide the 'Good Life for all'.

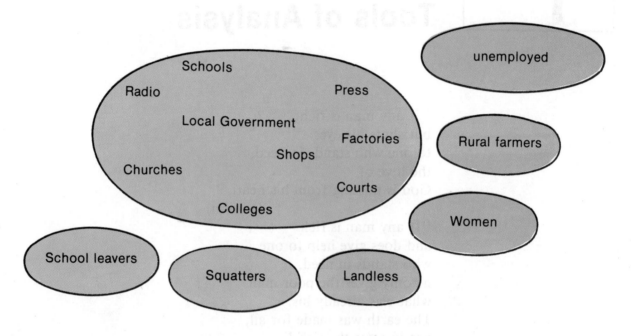

The Pyramid in Capitalist Society

Society is divided into three classes:

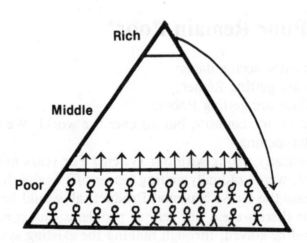

The aim of 'functional change' is to **take some of the wealth from the top** group, distribute it among the poor, so that they would become middle class, and 'all would be happy'.

For a while it seemed to some in the Western countries that this could be achieved. But by 1970, it was found that a bigger percentage of people were hungrier and poorer than in 1950 or 1960. This was not just due to natural disasters, like drought and famines in the Sahel and Ethiopia and floods in Bangladesh. The gap between rich and poor was clearly growing on a worldwide scale.

More serious questions were then raised:

— Was there something wrong at the basis of the whole structure?
— Did we need to go back to the roots of our system and see if we need structural changes?

Wealth Comes from Production

Originally people had their share of the means of production.

They had **raw materials**.

They worked and produced food. The bread belonged to the people because they had produced it. If they had more than they needed, they exchanged it for other things, e.g. clothes, which the other people had made.

With the development of Capitalism, One man became the owner.

The workers were now separated from their products.

> **The Products belonged to the Owner
> and not to the person who produced them.**

The 'Agricultural Revolution, as it was called, concentrated all the land in the hands of a few, so then the workers had no means to live, except to sell their labour (which meant themselves).

Rich people bought 'Labour' and 'Land', just like any other Things. The owner paid the worker a wage, sufficient for the essentials of life, enough to keep the worker and family alive. The surplus profit the owner kept for himself.

> All People Need Bread and Love.
> But is true Human Dignity and
> Love possible where one person is
> totally dependent on another for
> Daily Bread?

This separation of the workers from their production divided people into two classes:
— *The Owners* — Those with 'income-producing property,' such as land, machinery, factories, extra houses, from which they could make money,
— *The Non-Owners* — who had little or no property. They depended entirely on selling their labour for a living.

This division between those who can make money from property as well as from work, and those who can only make money by selling their labour, is still the basic division today. This is one of the major causes of the growing gap between the rich and the poor.

> **The poor man and the rich man
> do not play together.**
> — Ashanti proverb

Progress Means Profit in Capitalism

The key value of Capitalism is greater and greater profit. Progress means profit — the Worship of the Almighty Dollar. The chief commandment is 'Thou shalt Accumulate'.

It is private ownership of the means of production, i.e.:
— land,
— raw materials (oil, coal, minerals, cotton, etc.)
— tools,
— machines,
— factories, etc.

which causes the growing gap between the rich and the poor, not private ownership of property for personal use such as a home, a small farm, a bicycle, a car, etc.

Along with land, raw materials, and machinery, **labour** was itself, of course, one of the major factors of production. As technology developed, knowledge and skill became increasingly important, so those with education and special training had far greater security than those who had only their physical strength to offer in the labour market.

Apart from the Owners, many different classes have developed.

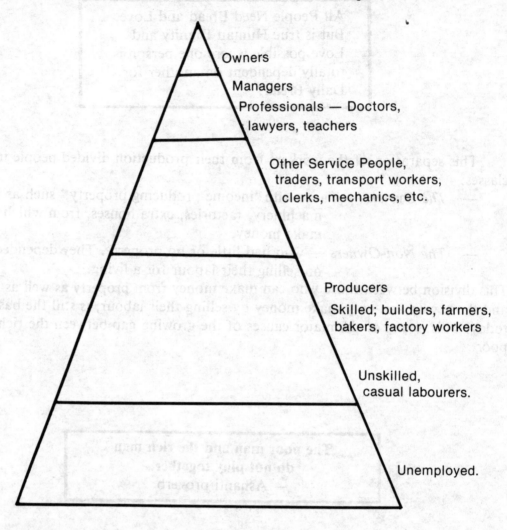

Owners

Managers

Professionals — Doctors, lawyers, teachers

Other Service People, traders, transport workers, clerks, mechanics, etc.

Producers

Skilled; builders, farmers, bakers, factory workers

Unskilled, casual labourers.

Unemployed.

The 'Promising' Period in the West

In capitalism the owners concentrate on 'Accumulation of Profits', keeping wages as low as possible. Profits are invested in bigger and better factories and machinery

    (a)   to compete with other factories and

    (b)   to make greater profits

Competition and expansion becomes the law of life.

> "We must sell more.
> We must advertise more.
> We must find more markets."

But capitalists realised after a number of strikes, that if wages were raised, the workers would **buy more** and this would increase the market. More money was paid especially to skilled workers, and they were able to buy more and raise their standard of living. Rapid advances in technology meant that so much was produced that there should have been plenty for everyone. For a time in the 50's and 60's in the western countries, it seemed as if all people could be drawn into the circle of prosperity, that poverty could be abolished.

Wages for some workers were good enough for them to feel that capitalism was to their advantage and they gave their loyalty to the capitalist system and the owners. But the marginal groups remained poor. Gradually they began to suspect that such a group, working only on a part-time basis at the bottom of the ladder, was needed to keep the whole hierarchical system firmly under the control of the group of owners.

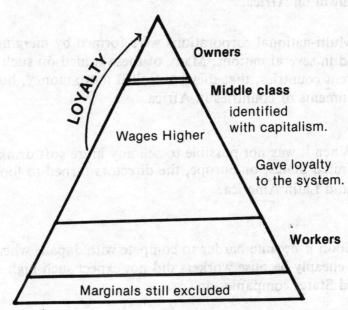

In the western countries, initially, wages were low. Then wages increased, but automation (machines doing work previously done by people) also increased, so many workers were dismissed and became unemployed. The State stepped in and provided 'Welfare for the Unemployed', to make sure they would still have money to buy the products of manufacturers.

The Age of Imperialism is the international expansion of capitalism especially after World War II. Competition for markets to sell goods manufactured got stronger and fiercer all the time. Every factory had to be constantly improving its machinery to produce goods more cheaply than other factories. Technology was constantly changing, and became like a race.

The factory with old-fashioned machinery could not produce enough goods cheaply enough to compete with a modern one and so was forced out of business. Small businesses collapsed, and rich and powerful firms took over control. They raised prices and were constantly searching for **cheap labour and foreign markets**.

CAPITALIST EXPANSION

Textile factories began to make clothing also. Factories became companies with many branches. Companies united and became corporations. The market in the home country became too small and directors looked overseas for more buyers of their goods.

Capitalist expansion internationally began in the early 19th century particularly in Asia. When Africa was partitioned between the capitalist countries, it spread to Africa. United States capitalism concentrated mainly on Latin America; European capitalism on Africa.

Multi-national corporations were formed by merging together smaller companies started in several nations. Many of these traded on such a huge scale in many different countries, that they controlled more money, buildings, etc. than many governments of countries in Africa.

When it was not possible to sell any more soft drinks or tyres or motor cars in the United States, or Europe, the directors turned to look for new markets in Africa, Asia and Latin America.

Soon it became harder to compete with Japan, where goods could be produced more cheaply because workers did not expect such high salaries. What could the United States companies do?

They set up factories in Asia, Africa and Latin America and used cheap local labour. In these countries, they needed a small, elite educated group to become joint owners and managers, and so a second pyramid grew beneath that in the United States.

Most profits return to the capitalist countries overseas. Wages in the Third World are not high enough for more than a few to buy the products, meanwhile other prices go up. Life becomes harder for the poor.

As factories move to the Third World, workers in the First World lose their jobs, leading to unemployment there. Under the present system, workers in both places suffer. Transnational corporations are concentrating more and more wealth in the hands of fewer and fewer people. Military power is used to protect business interests.

The folllowing diagram shows this relationship between First and Third World capitalism.

* See *How Europe Underdeveloped Africa* by Walter Rodney for a more detailed analysis.

The Double Triangle

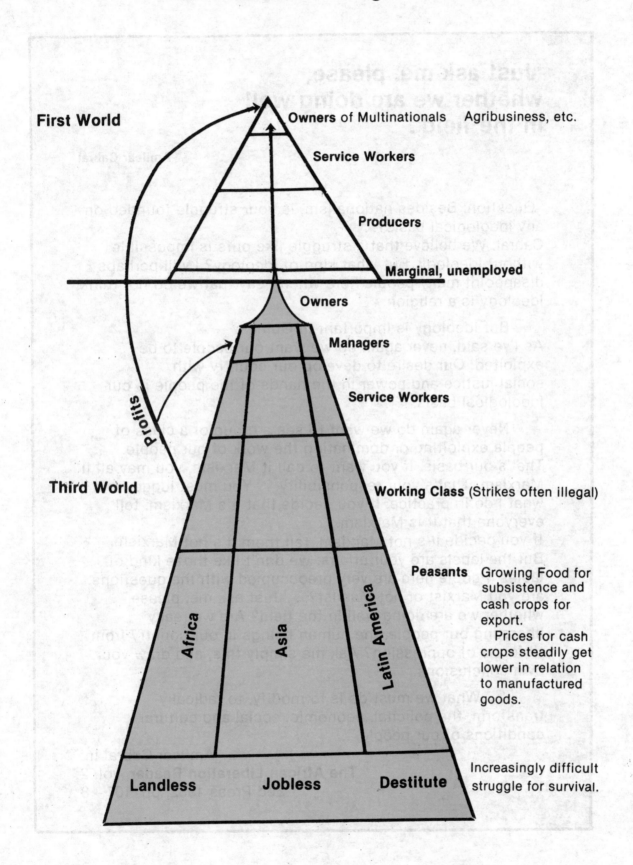

First World

Owners of Multinationals   Agribusiness, etc.

Service Workers

Producers

Marginal, unemployed

Owners

Managers

Service Workers

Profits

Third World

Working Class (Strikes often illegal)

Africa

Asia

Latin America

Peasants   Growing Food for subsistence and cash crops for export.
   Prices for cash crops steadily get lower in relation to manufactured goods.

Landless   **Jobless**   **Destitute**

Increasingly difficult struggle for survival.

'Just ask me, please, whether we are doing well in the field'.

Amilcar Cabral

"Question: Besides nationalism, is your struggle founded on any ideological basis?. . .
Cabral: We believe that a struggle like ours is impossible without ideology. But what kind of ideology? I will perhaps disappoint many people here when I say that we do not think ideology is a religion. . .

But ideology is important in Guinea.
As I've said, never again do we want our people to be exploited. Our desire to develop our country with social justice and power in the hands of the people is our ideological basis.

Never again do we want to see a group or a class of people exploiting or dominating the work of our people. That's our basis. If you want to call it Marxism, you may all it Marxism. That's your responsibility. . . You must judge from what I do in practice. If you decide that it's Marxism, tell everyone that it is Marxism.
If you decide it's not Marxism, tell them it's not Marxism. But the labels are your affairs; we don't like those kind of lables. People here are very preoccupied with the questions: are you Marxist or not Marxist?. . . Just ask me, please, whether we are doing well in the field? Are we really liberating our people, the human beings in our country from all forms of oppression? Ask me simply this, and draw your own conclusions.

". . .What we must do is to modify, to radically transform, the policital, economic, social and cultural conditions of our people."

Amilcar Cabral in:
The African Liberation Reader, vol. 2
Zed Press 1982, pp. 107 – 8

B. Ways to Look at Root Causes

In all community work, it is important to draw as many of the participants as possible into a process of critical reflection on what they are doing. The cycle of Action/Reflection/Action/ Reflection should involve everybody in the project.

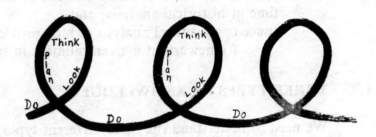

However, there will always be a smaller group ready and able to reflect on the situation and the actions taken, more frequently and at a deeper level. This group participates in a double cycle of reflection, with all the other participants and on their own. They play a very important role in determining the significance of the activity of the group and ensuring that it really is part of a liberating and transformative process.

This **double cycle of reflection** would look like this:

The following tools of analysis will probably be used mainly by such a group.

Analysis is not a mystery. We all try to do it as soon as we try to understand the root causes of our problems. But often we go round and round in circles, describing but not analysing.

Models can be extremely helpful in moving from description to analysis, in showing up the links between different issues and problems, in highlighting the system as a whole and not merely the different structures which we happen to encounter.

This in turn helps us to see the root causes of the problems and leads us towards strategies to deal with these problems. But we should always remember that a model is only a model; by simplifying, it brings things into perspective, like the focussing lenses on a pair of field glasses, but reality is always richer and more complex than the model.

Usually reality is so complex that 'we can't see the wood for the trees'. A model helps us to see, in a flash, 'the whole wood'.

Social analysis sometimes focuses on isolated **Issues,** such as hunger, unemployment or inflation. At other times it focuses on the **Policies** dealing with these issues. It might also focus on the economic, social, political and cultural **Structures** of a society, and ultimately it reaches beyond issues, policies and structures to the **System** in which all of these are inter-related.*

The social system needs to be analysed both in terms of:

time or historical analysis, and

space or structural analysis (which provides a cross-section of a system's framework at a given moment in time.)*

1.   THREE TYPES OF KNOWLEDGE

We need to understand the three different types of knowledge in order to come to critical awareness

Social knowledge is acquired by all people in the process of living. It is very valuable.

Scientific knowledge is based on a hypothesis which is solidly supported by facts. (A hypothesis is an insight into some aspect of truth.) Often scientific knowledge is highly specialised and deals with only a very small part of reality.

Transformative knowledge is formed through the interaction of social and scientific knowledge, as people together struggle to deepen their knowledge and change their situation. This is the type of knowledge needed within a whole community if they are to become the subjects of their own history (or to transform their lives, their communities, their world).

**Knowledge is like a garden:
if it is not cultivated,
it cannot be harvested.**

Guinean proverb

---

2.   MAIN STEPS OF ANALYSIS

a. **Observation**   What is happening?

We need to begin with an accurate description of the reality we seek to understand.

b. **Classification**

Which of the descriptions relate primarily to:

— survival or economics,

— decision-making or politics, or

— values and meaning or culture?

---

* Joe Holland and Peter Henriot, S.J., *Social Analysis Linking Faith and Justice*, Center of Concern, 3700 13th Street, N.E. Washington D.C. 20017, pp. 5 and 6.

c. **Inter-Relation** How are these facts related to each other?
The following short exercise can help people understand
this inter-relationship.
What is the meaning of this? I V I I I .Nothing.

Until we put if together like this:

d. **Insight** We see interrelationships.
What is cause or effect? What is important or relatively
unimportant?

e. **Causes** Here we examine why things interrelate; structures, cause, situations.
But situations/people also change structures.

f. **Hypothesis**
We draw up a hypothesis as to why things happen and
how to bring about change. The verification of our
hypothesis is a positive response to the question:
does it work?

3. SHAPE OF THE WORLD* — AN EXERCISE ON OBSERVATION

This is a very stimulating exercise which helps a group to share their perceptions of the most important things happening in the world. It develops interest in the forces which are changing the world, for better or for worse.

If members of the group come from very different backgrounds, the sharing can stretch people's insights through the variety of perceptions. It may be advisable to do a listening exercise before starting, to ensure that people try to understand each other's point of view. If it is done in this spirit, it can lay a basis of trust in a very diverse group and provide a common experience for many types of analysis.

Procedure

Ask the participants to form mixed groups of fives and then to sit around tables where newsprint, markers, crayons and individual papers are provided. The facilitator explains that there are five steps in the exercise. Each step is explained, one at a time and the facilitator illustrates each step on newsprint on the wall.

1. Main Illustration.
   a. Ask each person to draw a circle on a plain piece of paper. Explain that this circle represents the world in which the participants live.
   b. Ask, "If you could draw a picture (or a symbol) of the world, what would be its main illustration (its main theme)?" Give time for each person to make their own drawing on a separate sheet of paper.
   c. Ask each person to share what they were trying to express in their drawing in their small group.
   d. Then ask each group to make a common picture on newsprint including everyone's idea. Either plan together a new drawing which includes all the ideas or draw different ideas in different parts of the circle. (Warn them not to draw the circle on newsprint too large, or to draw outside the circle, since they will have to use the outer space for arrows later.)

* MDI Group, 1975

15

2.   **Future New Impacts**

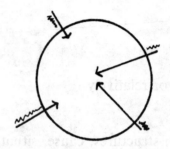

a. Ask each small group now to discuss: "What do you believe is having an impact on the world now, and over the next few years will continue to affect it strongly?

b. Show this by putting arrows into the circle and labelling them. Arrows directly into the centre show the most direct impact while arrows not into the centre describe a less direct impact.

3.   **Influences Dying-Out in the Future**

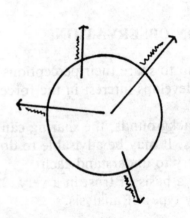

a. When the small groups have finished the above task, ask each small group: "What things are dying out in the world now or will continue to do so in the next few years?

b. Again they do this by using arrows going out of the circle and labelling them. Arrows leaving from the centre represent important influences dying out while arrows leaving from less central parts of the circle describe weaker influences fading away.

4.   **Long-Range Impact**

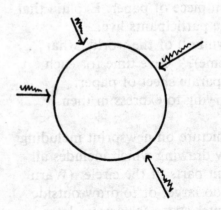

a. When the small groups have finished the above task, ask each group, "What things do you believe will one day have an impact on the world but which are now five or ten years, or more, away?"

b. Show these by arrows adjacent to the circle and label them.

5.   Implications

   a.   When all the above tasks are completed, ask each person to reflect
        quietly and write:
        "What is the major insight this process has given me?" (Or, what does
        this mean to me and our group?)

   b.   After about 5 minutes of quiet time, ask the small groups to discuss
        their points and then write on newsprint a summary of the insights and
        implications they have discussed.

   c.   Share these implications in the whole group. This can be a very useful
        basis for further work in the group.
             Each group is asked to put up their newsprint and the group can
        then walk around looking at each newsprint, asking questions as they
        go.

Time   About 2½ to 3 hours.

Materials   Newsprint, markers, crayons, tape, individual paper, tables for groups to
work at.

C.   Tools of Analysis

In this section we present just a few of the models which groups have found most helpful to observe, classify and inter-relate their knowledge as a basis for planning transformative action. In all of these the poor and oppressed provide the perspective from which we start to analyse a situation. The use of these models has led the authors and many of those in groups we have worked with, to a strong conviction that capitalist imperialism is doing untold harm to the poor in Africa and that a just society requires some form of African socialism. We hope that the use of these models will help groups to clarify what is needed and how it needs to be done.

Behind each model lies a great deal of research, and those wanting more background should consult the bibliography.

1.   The Poor as our Perspective — Structural Analysis[1]

"Structural analysis becomes a crucially important tool for awareness-building among the poor and oppressed. It involves a dynamic process where the awareness of the oppressed people is articulated and acted upon in the context of their own active programs. This enables these people to take their history into their own hands and to move forward. It is this progression which enables a program to become a people's movement."

The goal of structural analysis is to rectify previous development methodology which failed to achieve a true development process — i.e. people who become truly independent, standing straight on their own feet, actively participating in decision-making and becoming activators of their own future, contributing to society as a whole.

To accomplish this, analysis needs to reveal the character of the system of the society, to uncover a system of bondage in order to transform the power structure in a process of liberation.

2.   Levels of Awareness[2]

a.   "Micro" (small scale). The process of structural analysis must start with the people; with their local situation — family — the village — the place of work — the trade union — the minority groups (ethnic and religious) where the people live and work. They must undertake the analysis themselves.

b.   "Macro" (large scale). The local situation is usually determined by the impact of the whole system of society upon it. Hence, a second level of structural analysis is imperative. This needs to be undertaken by those who are committed to the cause of the poor and will therefore find the resources to meet these needs. **The role of the animator is to bring together these two levels of analysis in the midst of the people.**

1. Reprinted from *Guidelines for Development*, edited by Harvey L. Perkins, by permission of Christian Conference of Asia, 480 Lorong 2, Toa Payoah, Singapore 1231, 1980, p. 52.
2. Op. cit. p. 53.

3.   Clarifying Statement*

"Without an adequate analysis, a program may inadvertently operate within the broader framework of an exploitative system, and even help to strengthen and augment the forces of oppression."

> Development with social justice can take place only when we are clear where injustice is taking place.

---

4.   Tools of Analysis*

"Social analysis involves two sets of relationships:
— between classes. This is class analysis.
— between the sub-systems of society.
There are three basic sub-systems:
    a. economic,
    b. political,
    c. cultural (including religion, family, education, mass media).
This is structural analysis and covers both how they operate in themselves and how they relate."

Summary

Therefore, one can see several stages for the development of critical awareness:

Stage 1. Building Involvement at Grassroots
Breaking through the 'culture of silence'.

Stage 2. Systematic Observation
People identifying root causes of oppression.

Stage 3. Structural Analysis
Revealing the links of the system.

Stage 4. Setting Goals
Providing an overall perspective in relation to the structures in the local/national situation.

Stage 5. Strategy and Tactics
Planning and implementing actions.

Stage 6. Ongoing Reflection and Action.

---

* Op. cit. p. 55.

5. **THE THREE STOREY BUILDING**

Values and Beliefs (Cultural)

These are expressed and passed on through the education system, radios, newspapers, traditions and customs.

This level **justifies** the society and makes it feel respect for itself.

Organisation (Political)

All societies develop laws and methods of enforcing these laws (through councils, parliament, courts, police, army, prisons). The group that becomes dominant at the social and economic level controls decisions at this level.

The laws passed can serve the interests of the dominant class.

They can help to provide for the fundamental needs of all and they can prevent these needs being met.

This level **organises** the society.

Survival (Economic and Social)

All people need FOOD and LOVE. BREAD and DIGNITY.
To get these we need to overcome FAMINE and ISOLATION.
We seek Production and Reproduction (family).

To produce one needs Raw Materials, Tools and Work. The way a society meets its needs forms the basis on which the society is built. The mode of production and the social relations involved provide the key which unlocks the nature of that social system.

This level **conditions** society.

An Exercise to Begin Structural Analysis

We usually presented this model to a group before they began work on more detailed local analysis.

Procedure

a. Begin with the economic level using questions and filling in the blocks on a large piece of newsprint.

b. Start with the base and move from the bottom up.

Economic and Social Level

— What are the chief means of production?
— Who owns them?
— Who works?
— What is the mode of production? (What type of arrangement is there between who works for whom? Is it feudal, capitalistic?)
— Who controls distribution of goods? How?
— What different classes emerge from the mode of production?
— What are the relationships between the different classes?
— What effect does this have on relationships in families, different tribes, other groups, etc.?

Organisation Level (Political)

— Who has the power to make decisions?
— From which class are they?
— Who makes the laws?
— For whose benefit are they made?
— How are the laws enforced?

Beliefs and Values (Cultural)

— What does the society believe about itself?
— What are its chief values?
— Are the 'expressed values' and the actual values the same?
— Who promotes official values? How?

c. Ask the group to reflect on their answers which have now been written on newsprint.

1. What **links** do you see between the different levels?
2. How is the economic situation influencing the legal and political level?
3. How do these two levels influence the level of values?
4. How are the real values and the expressed values of the people influencing the political and the economic levels?

d. Ask the group to study and fill in a copy of the diagram on the opposite page, giving practical examples from the situation they know best.

e. After discussion on the links people see between the different levels, it can be useful to share the meaning of 'dialectical relationship'. Sometimes it is best to use a second piece of newsprint leaving the three blocks empty, then drawing and labelling an arrow for each link, identified by the group.

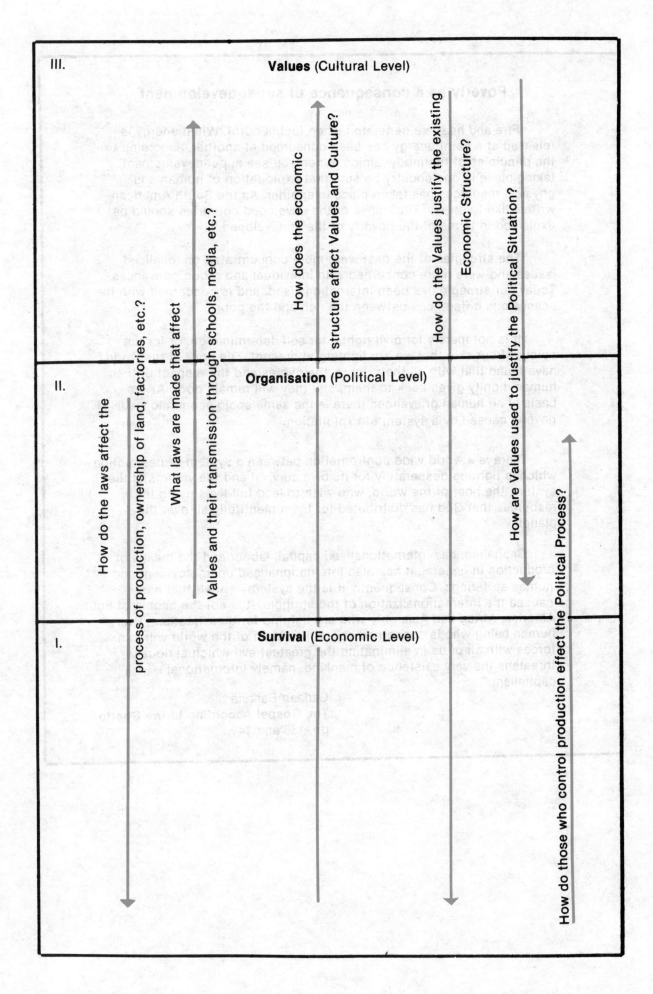

III. **Values** (Cultural Level)

How does the economic structure affect Values and Culture?

How do the Values justify the existing Economic Structure?

II. **Organisation** (Political Level)

What laws are made that affect Values and their transmission through schools, media, etc.?

How do the laws affect the process of production, ownership of land, factories, etc.?

How are Values used to justify the Political Process?

I. **Survival** (Economic Level)

How do those who control production effect the Political Process?

Poverty as a consequence of super-development

"Fire and heat are generated when fuel is burnt. When energy is released at a point energy has been consumed at another, according to the principles of thermodynamics. When you see super-development taking place in one country be sure that exploitation of human and physical resources has taken place in another. As the South American writers like to stress: The riches of the developed countries should be explained in terms of the poverty of the undeveloped."

"The struggles of the past were more concentrated on localised issues and were more concerned with individual and group grievances. Today our struggle has been internationalised, and is concerned with the scandalous differences between the rich and the poor. . . ."

"It is not merely for civil rights, for self-determination, or for the colour of our skin that we are fighting at present. The poor of the world have found that with all their rights, their votes and the respect of their human dignity given back to them, still they will remain poor. At the basis of all human grievances there is the same socio-economic issue of poverty caused by a system of exploitation.

There is a world wide confrontation between a system of destruction which is fighting desperately for its own survival and the victims of the system, the poor of the world, who wish to lead full lives using the resources that God has distributed for them plentifully all over the planet.

Capitalism has internationalised capital, labour and the means of production in general. It has also internationalised unemployment and human sufferings. Consequently it is the system itself that has caused the internationalization of the struggle. It is not the people of South America, Africa and Asia only who are fighting for their freedom. Every human being who is concerned about the future of the world will join forces with all of us in eliminating the greatest evil which seriously threatens the very existence of mankind, namely international capitalism."

Canaan Banana
The Gospel According to the Ghetto
pp. 136 and 141.

D.   Starting to Understand Simple Economics[1]

> **Economics
> is about People,
> their Life
> and their Work.**

1.   THE CENTRE PERIPHERY MODEL[2]

This model illustrates the insights of Andre Gundar Frank, that underdevelopment is not a natural situation. **Underdevelopment is created** by the

current economic system which sucks resources from the rural areas to the towns, from towns to capital cities, from third world countries to the financial capitals of industrialised nations (New York, London, Frankfurt, Tokyo, etc.) the headquarters of the transnational corporations. (These are sometimes hidden in small islands like the Bahamas where they can escape taxation.)

This model can be used as a summary on many different levels. Rural people without much formal education can understand the first level, after playing the Rural Money Game[3] and discussing how the money earned in their own area is constantly sucked back into the district, town, and from there goes to the capital city.

2.   EXERCISE: WHERE DOES OUR MONEY GO?

A simple introduction to this model is to show a number of items that people in the village buy regularly (e.g. bottle of Coca-Cola, beer, pair of shoes, trousers, dress or cloth, aspirin, cement blocks, roofing, tools etc. Then ask:

> "When we buy these things, where does the money go?"

---

1. For further information about this model see Andre Gundar Frank, *Dependent Accumulation and Underdevelopment*, Monthly Review Press.
2. This chapter has been mainly adapted from models and insights from INODEP, the Ecumenical Institute for the Development of People — (Paris).
3. For complete instructions for Rural Money Game see DELTA Handbook 1, p. 169.

First Level

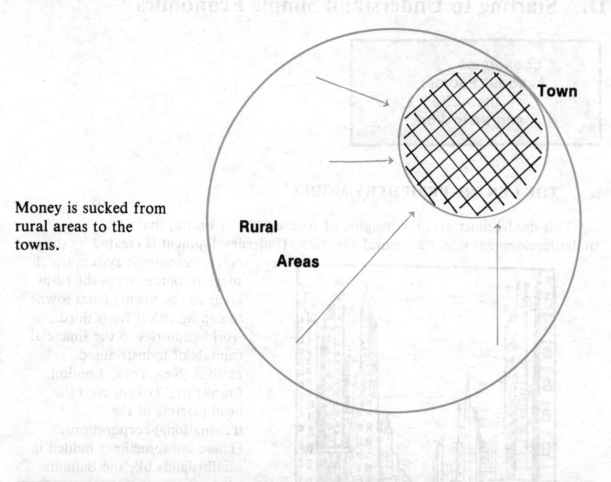

Money is sucked from rural areas to the towns.

Town

Rural Areas

"How can we keep more of the money circulating in our own area?

This is the basic question of self-reliance on every level:-

— the village
— the district
— the nation
— the region.

Second Level

This can be used after a field trip to visit a factory owned by a Multi-National Corporation, such as Bata Shoes, Brooke Bond Tea, etc. It can also be used after discussion on a film such as 'The Dispossessed', '5 Billion People', or 'Growing Dollars'.

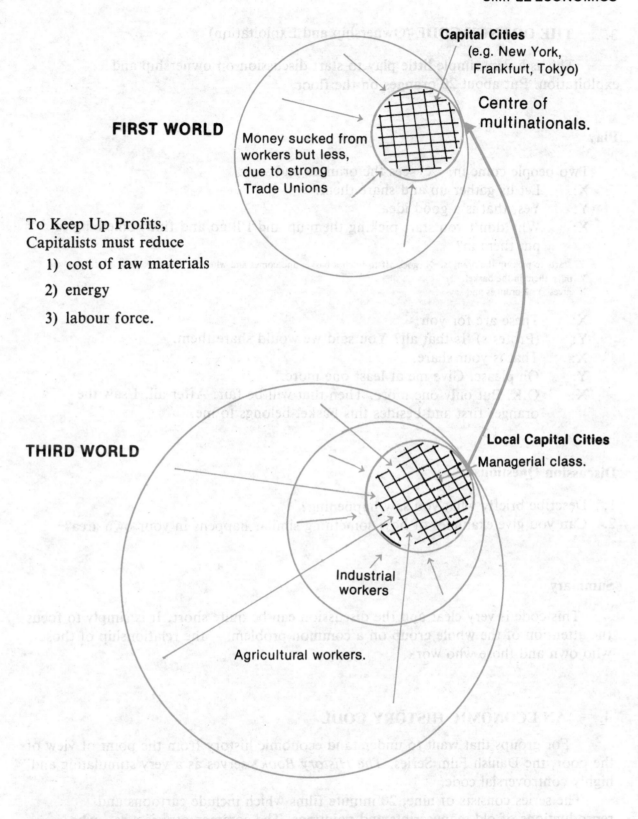

FIRST WORLD

Capital Cities
(e.g. New York,
Frankfurt, Tokyo)

Centre of
multinationals.

Money sucked from
workers but less,
due to strong
Trade Unions

To Keep Up Profits,
Capitalists must reduce
    1) cost of raw materials
    2) energy
    3) labour force.

THIRD WORLD

Local Capital Cities
Managerial class.

Industrial
workers

Agricultural workers.

**The person who is being carried does not
realize how far the town is.**

— Nigerian proverb

3.   **THE ORANGE CODE** (Ownership and Exploitation)

This is a very simple little play to start discussion on ownership and exploitation. Put about 20 oranges on the floor.

Play

Two people come in. X sees the oranges and says:

X: Let us gather up and share them.

Y: Yes, that is a good idea.

X: Why don't you start picking them up and I'll go and find something to put them in?

Y starts to pick up the oranges. X goes off to fetch a basket and comes and when Y has picked up all the oranges, Y puts them in the basket.
X gives Y 2 oranges and says:

X: These are for you.

Y: (Protests) 'Is that all? You said we would share them.'

X: That is your share.

Y: Oh please. Give me at least one more.

X: O.K. But only one more. Then that will be fair. After all, I saw the oranges first and besides this basket belongs to me.

Discussion Questions

1. Describe briefly what you saw happening?
2. Can you give examples of how something similar happens in your own area?

Summary

This code is very clear and the discussion can be quite short. It is simply to focus the attention of the whole group on a common problem — the relationship of those who own and those who work.

4.   **AN ECONOMIC HISTORY CODE**

For groups that want to understand economic history from the point of view of the poor, the Danish Film Series, *The History Book** serves as a very stimulating and highly controversial code.

The series consists of nine, 20 minute films which include cartoons and reproductions of old manuscripts and paintings. The commentator is a rat, who expresses his justifiable anger towards the capitalist system in unpleasantly shrill tones, which at times unnecessarily provokes resistance. The series begins with feudalism, shows the development of the merchant traders, early capitalism, the effects of the slave trade on both Africa and the West, and the rise of the finance capitalist, 19th Century opposition from workers and the repression by the capitalist class. The last three films of the series, on Russia, Imperialism and Guinea Bissau are rather disappointing.

* Distributed by Unifilm, 419 Park Avenue South, New York, N.Y. 10016 USA.

Though some may dislike certain aspects of these films, we find that people remember them years after they have seen them and affirm that they played a very important role in laying a foundation for their understanding of economics.

An animator should certainly preview them before using them to see if they are suitable for a particular group and then work out appropriate questions for the group on each film.

5.   FOUR MAIN TYPES OF PRODUCTION

The following simple explanation of the types of production is important in understanding the social relationships between owners and workers.

Four Main Types of Production

TYPE OF PRODUCTION

Ownership of land, factories, machines, etc.	Labour	Rural	Industrial
1. A owns	B works for A	A is a Landowner	A is a Factory Owner
2. A owns and	A works and A employs B	A is a Rich Peasant	A is a Small Businessman
3. A owns and	A works	A is a Subsistence Farmer	A is a Craftsman
4. A does **not** own	A works for another, C, and 'sells his labour'	A is a Landless, Agricultural Labourer	A is a Factory Worker

Question

In your area, which is the most common type of production? Give examples of each kind.

Summary

The capitalist economy only starts when things are made, not primarily for use, but for profit. One system is changed for another as it reaches the limit of its ability to motivate people to produce more. This can be shown like this:

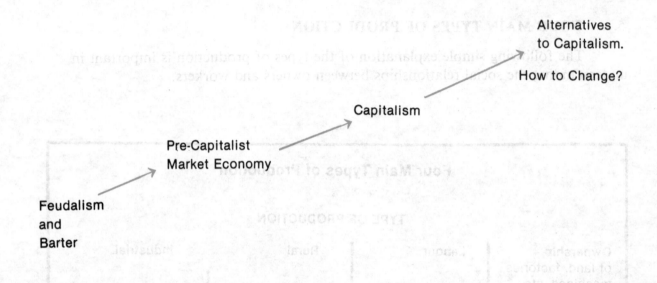

Alternatives
to Capitalism.

How to Change?

Capitalism

Pre-Capitalist
Market Economy

Feudalism
and
Barter

6.   WHAT IS EXPLOITATION?   Labour Value

Why are the Rich getting Richer and the Poor Poorer?
Where does Wealth come from?

Wealth comes from the additional value we give to raw materials by transforming them with Labour. Therefore the Value of Goods should be computed in Labour Time. (How many hours work to pay for: food, rent, clothes, etc.)

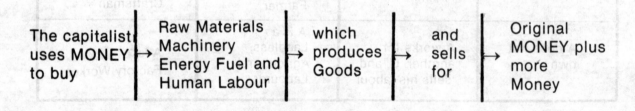

| The capitalist uses MONEY to buy | → | Raw Materials Machinery Energy Fuel and Human Labour | → | which produces Goods | → | and sells for | → | Original MONEY plus more Money |

(1)   If we take the Money made each day, and subtract Expenditure on
Raw Materials
plus machinery (factory investment and upkeep)
plus energy fuel,
we are left with the Value of the Goods Produced.

(2)   If we divide the Value of the Goods Produced (answer from
above), by the number of hours of Human Labour,
we find the Value of one person's work for one hour.

(3)   Compare this with the Wages paid for 8 hours work.
Very often the worker is paid the value of one hour's work when
(s)he has worked 8 hours.

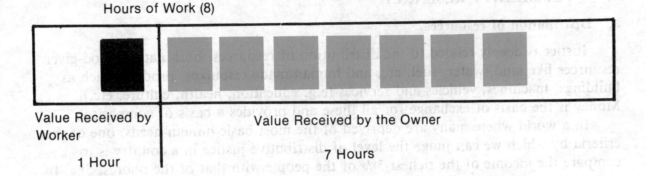

Hours of Work (8)

Value Received by Worker

Value Received by the Owner

1 Hour

7 Hours

Research has shown that in some situations the Daily Wage is as little as the value of 16 minutes work.

	Income	Expenditure	Value of Work	Wages	Hours Paid
e.g.	From Sales $150.00	Raw Materials Machinery $70 Fuel	$80 Surplus	$10 Value	1/8 = $70.00

Often when Workers strike for more pay the Managers show them books 'proving' that if they are paid more the firm will go bankrupt. (The workers almost feel obliged to take up a collection to save the firm!)

But if they can work out the value of their work in Labour Time, they can say to management, "You are only paying us for 1 hour's work. What is happening to the other 7 hours? If you cannot explain, there's something wrong with you."

In all systems, workers produce more than they get back. Of course the full value of Labour can never be paid out to workers. All forms of development depend on the production of Surplus Value. The important question is:

"Who decides how the surplus value shall be spent?
Even in a socialist mode of production,
where wages may be set above survival level,
there will still be the need for some surplus —
for reinvestment to build new factories,
— for taxes to provide social services,
education, medical services, etc.

But who controls decision-making of how this surplus will be spent? This is one of the main meeting points of Economics and Politics.

Examples of Local Industrial Research

A Mauritian Sugar Labourer was paid 10c per hour.
Has to pay 55c for 1 pound of sugar.
Therefore has to work 5½ hours for 1 pound sugar.
A woman in Taiwan has to sew 80 pairs of blue jeans
to earn enough to buy 1 pair of jeans.

Especially in Trade Union Negotiations, workers need to change the ground on which they bargain, from **Money** to **Labour Value**, to show clearly the Basis of Exploitation.

31

7.   COMMUNITY RESEARCH

a.   Distribution of resources.

Justice is deeply related to the distribution of resources, both natural God-given resources like land, water, fuel, etc. and human-made resources, products such as buildings, machines, vehicles and services (e.g. education, health, culture, etc.). Money is the basis of exchange for all these and provides a basis of comparison.

In a world where many are deprived of the most basic human needs, one of the criteria by which we can judge the level of distributive justice in a country is to compare the income of the richest 5% of the people with that of the poorest 5%. In some African countries the **richest 5% earn 52 times** as much as the poorest 5%. In some socialist countries (e.g. Romania) the rich receive only 6 times as much as the poor. If we are struggling for a more just distribution of wealth, we need to know the situation in our own country.

Appropriate Guidelines for Research need to be worked out in each situation. One always needs to begin with the small scale situation most familiar to the participants.

b.   Local research

Even on the village level people can be involved in Community Research, and it can form an important part of the process of conscientization.

Indicators (Signs of Wealth and Class). The group can brainstorm answers to this question:

(1)   What are the most important signs of wealth in the community? (E.g. size of farm, type of house, cars, bicycles, carts, cattle, etc.)

(2)   How many in our area (clear boundaries chosen) have each of these?

(3)   What are the most important signs of poverty? (E.g. no food, no land, no cows, poor or crowded housing, children unable to go to school, distance from water and clinics, etc.)

(4)   How many in our area suffer from these problems? As in all problem-posing education, the process must continue with the questions:

(5)   What are the causes of these problems?

(6)   What can we do about them?

c.   Local and international analysis

We include here 2 questionnaires from the Asian Handbook, **Guidelines for Development,** for research on the small scale familiar situation and for research on the wider level, which affect every local situation.

Obviously these questionnaires **need to be adapted for every different situation** and they are given here simply as guidelines from which to make your own questionnaire.

It is very important for the animator to help the group find the sources of the information they require, and if necessary to find an outside resource person, such as a librarian who can do this. Nearly all governments do a lot of research as a basis for their development planning and in most cases, this is available in the form of Statistical Digests, and other publications from government printers or university Development Institutes.

Again, it is a question of not losing sight of the wood because of the trees. Too many statistics confuse the picture rather than clarifying the situation. Some group needs to decide what are the significant facts we need to find out and give guidelines about how these facts can be presented visually to the whole group as the basis for discussion.

> **Not to know is bad;**
> **not to wish to know is worse.**
> — Nigerian proverb

8. A Guide for Local Analysis*

Class Analysis and Methods of Exploitation.
1. Who are the landlords?
2. What do they produce?
3. What are the sizes of their landholdings?
4. What is the extent of their economic power?
5. Status of the landlords: rich, middle, absentee, etc.
6. How do the landlords exploit the poor peasants and the farm workers?
7. To what extent do the landlords engage in exploitation?

Problems for a thorough Land Reform
1. Is land distribution necessary? No. Yes. Why?
2. Is the reduction of rent possible? No. Yes. Why?
3. Are the farm managers and the landlords themselves cruel and oppressive to the workers? No. Yes. How?
4. Can a co-operative without landlords and rich peasants be created? Yes. No. Why?
5. Is the local government in any position to extend credit, extension service and others to the local peasant despite its heavy commitment elsewhere? No. Yes. Why?
6. What can the poor peasants and farmers do to protect their economic and political gains?
7. Is Land Reform being applied? If yes, how? If no, why?
8. To what extent can it be used to alleviate the plight of the poor?
9. To what extend are the landlords free from the Land Reform regulations?
10. Is there a code or law about the land reform? Does it favour the landlords themselves?

Problems of the Workers
1. Are the wages of the workers sufficient for their decent maintenance?
2. Are the wages in step with the profits of the company or plantation?
3. If there is a union, what must be done to strengthen it or to transform it to a good one?
4. If there is none, what must be done to create one?
5. Is the company or plantation repressive or oppressive against the workers? If yes, how?
6. How inefficient or ineffective are any legal provisions to protect workers?
7. What are the present violations of these provisions which the people may work at?

---

* Asian Christian Conference, *Guidelines for Development*, pp. 58 – 61.

9. A Guide for Macro-Analysis

The Economic System.

1. **Production**
   a. How does society organise itself for material subsistence?
   b. What is produced? Agricultural or industrial? For local consumption or export crops?
   c. Where are the centres of production?
   d. Who owns the means of production? Are they owned privately or collectively? Where are the owners to be found, in the urban or in the rural sector?
   e. What kind of economic system is involved? Clan-based, Feudal, Capitalist, Socialist?

2. **Distribution**
   a. Is there a surplus? Is it real or artificial?
   b. How is the surplus distributed? Where are the points of distribution?
   c. What are the roles of these points of distribution? Do they allocate supplies, fix prices, etc.?
   d. Who controls the distribution points?

3. **Consumption**
   a. Is it a subsistence or a surplus economy?
   b. Who consumes the surplus and where are they located?

4. **Other Questions**
   a. Where does the economic activity take place? Urban or rural?
   b. Does the economic initiative come from outside the area or from within the area? Is the stimulus exterior and foreign or is it interior and national?
   c. Is there a dominant sector and a dependent sector within the economy? How is the rural dependent on the urban sector?

10. VISUAL PRESENTATIONS OF RESEARCH AS 'CODES'

In Africa, we have found that in the great majority of groups, a diagram provides a far better problem-posing code, and a basis for discussion than a written article. It also helps groups to internalise and grasp the significance of the facts they have read if they are asked to present these in visual diagramatic forms.

a. Circles and pies

These are particularly good for showing percentage distribution. E.g.
— production,
— population groups,
— ownership of land.

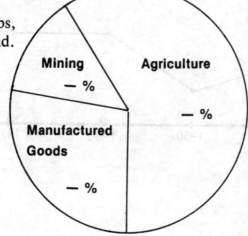

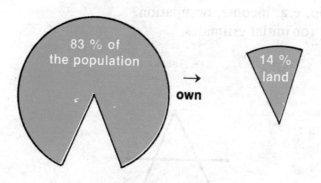

b. Block graphs

These are a very vivid way of drawing attention to a comparison between two related figures.

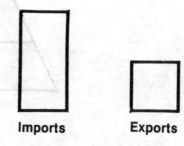

c. **Graphs**

These are helpful in showing trends over a number of years.

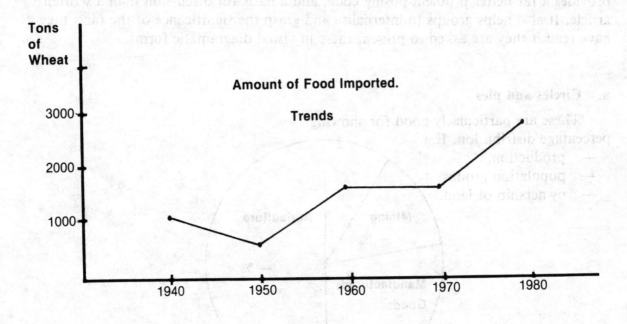

Amount of Food Imported.

Trends

d. **Triangles** are very good for showing a
hierarchical relationship, e.g. income, occupation.
This is especially good for initial estimates.

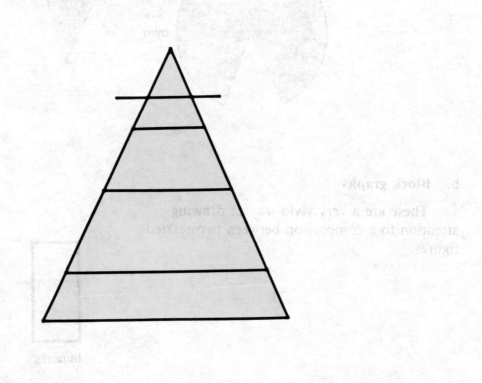

e. **The Lorentz Curve** is the best way of showing accurately the distribution of income or land. The deeper the curve, the **more unequal** the distribution. The other side of the triangle can be used to compare this income curve with land, or used to repeat the income curve to make a more vivid presentation.

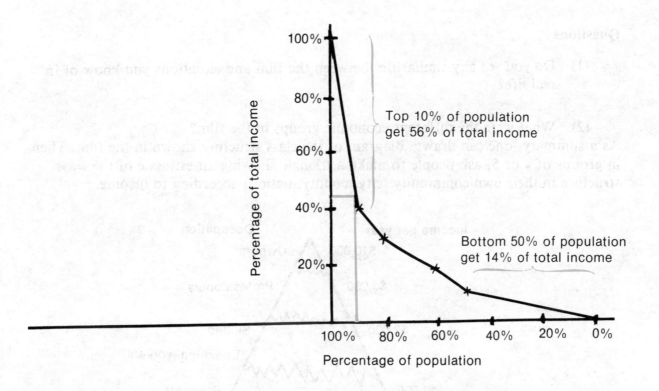

f. **Maps** are very important to show Population Density, resources, services (schools, hospitals, transport).

People need help about finding information, most of which is available. It is helpful to discuss what people are interested in knowing, and then present only a few of the most striking statistics.

These presentations can be used as codes, leading to discussion:

— What do you see happening?
— Why is it happening?
— What can we do about it on the local level?

11. CLASS ANALYSIS

Code   The film '1001 Hands' (see Book One page 137) about a carpet factory in Morocco, can be an excellent code to begin the discussion on class analysis. This film is so moving that one must first give the group an opportunity to discuss the things that struck them most powerfully.

Questions

(1)   Do you see any similarities between the film and situations you know of in real life?

(2)   What were the different economic groups in the film?

As a summary, one can draw a diagram of the class structure shown in the film. Then in groups of 4 or 5, ask people to make a triangle showing an estimate of the class structure in their own community (city, county, nation) according to income.

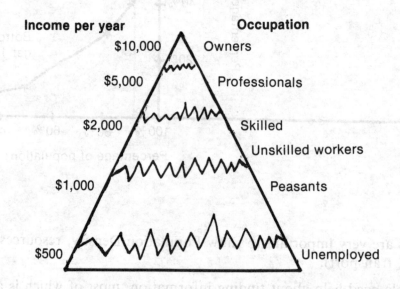

List the incomes on the left side and the occupations on the right hand side. It is usually necessary to make jagged horizontal lines to show that some skilled workers must earn more than some auxiliary class workers, e.g. teacher, civil servants.

E. Organisation for Decision-Making. Political Analysis

"Who makes, or influences, the decisions that affect the lives
of the people in a society?"

This is the most fundamental political question. The possibility of everybody sharing in this process, usually through elected representatives, is the basis of democracy, but history shows that even in situations where there is 'One Person / One Vote', there are other forces influencing or controlling the decisions and we need to understand these forces.

1. The Dynamic Model

This model of how the structures of society operate and interact has proved helpful to groups involved in the struggle for a just society in many different countries. It should be explained step by step, either drawing the model on a double sheet of newsprint or sticking up slips of paper with each block of words in the appropriate position on the wall.

Explanation of Dynamic Model

1. We begin at the bottom with the Economic Base of society — the Mode of Production.
2. From this base, the three classes emerge: Dominant, Auxiliary, and Subordinate.
3. Each class produces a group of leaders who can express and communicate the interests of their class and organise the people to ensure that these interests are met.
4. The Dominant class creates the State.
5. The State includes:
   — the Ideological Structure
   (schools, mass media, churches, political parties, cultural organisations, family set up) which propagates **the values and beliefs** of the Dominant class.
6. — and the Political Structure
   (parliament, congress, councils, laws, courts, military, police, prisons, etc.)
7. The Ideological Structure has its agents: (teachers, journalists, editors, broadcasters, extension officers, etc.)
8. The Political Structure has its agents.
   (M.P.'s, senators, judges, magistrates, lawyers, policemen, prison wardens, etc.)
   Both groups form part of the Auxiliary class, helping to promote the goals of the Dominant class.
9. The Dominant class uses the Ideological Structure to spread its Values, Beliefs (and myths) to the whole population.
   The more a society accepts the ideology of the dominant Class, the less pressure is necessary. Every society tries to work as much as possible through persuasion (i.e. education and propaganda) rather than force. Then there is 'peace and stability', that is, acceptance of the 'status quo'.

10. However, when the contradictions become intolerable, and the level of awareness of the Subordinate class rises, the persuasion is no longer effective.

    The State then uses the Political Structure to maintain control, passing tougher laws, making more use of police, prisons and the army. When the situation is firmly in control, the State returns to the practice of persuasion.

    Reflection on many situations shows a constant swing between persuasion and force.

11. The leaders of both the Auxiliary and the Subordinate classes often acquire certain privileges through education and ability. They can be strongly drawn to support the values and structures of the 'status quo'. (Note the positive sign ' + ' on the chart.)

    However they **can make an option**. They can choose to identify with the struggle of the oppressed to change the structures radically, and create a New Society. This is what Amilcar Cabral called class suicide. (Note the negative sign on chart.)

    The leadership of the Dominated classes usually emerges **not as individuals** but as groups, and in the process of struggle, they try to invent a new society — an alternative to the present situation.

    The leaders of the Auxiliary classes can make an important contribution, if they work with the oppressed, to help them analyse their situation and plan strategy.

    But they need to realise:

    a. that there will be a constant tension within them. The values of their class origin will still influence them, and often these will not coincide with the interests of the oppressed.

    b. that they can never create a new society on their own. Only to the extent that they are genuinely involved with a movement of the workers can they make a creative contribution to building a just new society.

12. Together with the workers, the leaders who have made a genuine option for the poor, can help set up alternative structures, which challenge, and hopefully supplant, first the ideological and then the political structures.

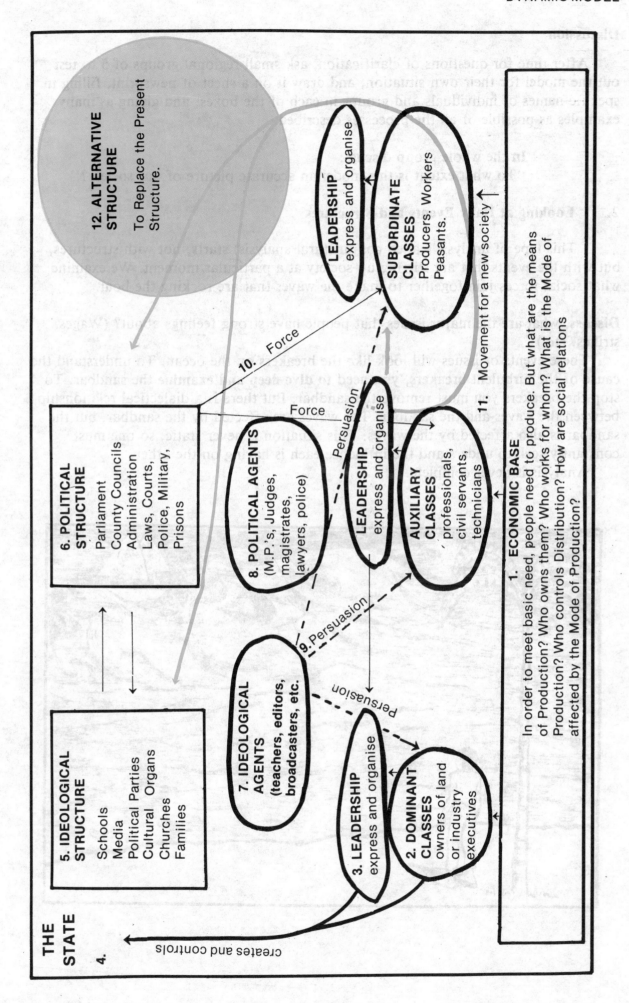

THE STATE

4.

creates and controls

5. IDEOLOGICAL STRUCTURE

Schools
Media
Political Parties
Cultural Organs
Churches
Families

6. POLITICAL STRUCTURE

Parliament
County Councils
Administration
Laws, Courts,
Police, Military,
Prisons

7. IDEOLOGICAL AGENTS
(teachers, editors, broadcasters, etc.)

8. POLITICAL AGENTS
(M.P.'s, Judges, magistrates, lawyers, police)

3. LEADERSHIP express and organise

2. DOMINANT CLASSES
owners of land or industry executives

LEADERSHIP express and organise

AUXILIARY CLASSES
professionals, civil servants, technicians

LEADERSHIP express and organise

SUBORDINATE CLASSES
Producers. Workers Peasants.

12. ALTERNATIVE STRUCTURE
To Replace the Present Structure.

9. Persuasion

Persuasion

Persuasion

10. Force

Force

11. Movement for a new society

1. ECONOMIC BASE

In order to meet basic need, people need to produce. But what are the means of Production? Who owns them? Who works for whom? What is the Mode of Production? Who controls Distribution? How are social relations affected by the Mode of Production?

41

Discussion

After time for questions of clarification, ask small regional groups of 5 to test out the model for their own situation, and draw it on a sheet of newsprint, filling in specific names of individuals and groups in each of the boxes, and giving as many examples as possible of all the processes described.

In the whole group discuss:
"To what extent is this model an accurate picture of our society?"

2.   Looking at Daily Events and Structures

This type of analysis (called conjunctural analysis) starts, not with structures, but with the events that are stirring up society at a particular moment. We examine what social forces join together to make the waves that are rocking the boat.

Discuss, what are the major issues that people have strong feelings about? (Wages, strikes, etc.)

These events or issues will look like the breakers on the ocean. To understand the cause of the turbulent breakers, you need **to dive deep and examine** the sandbar. To stop the breakers you must remove the sandbar. But there is a dialectical relationship between the waves and the sandbar. The waves are affected by the sandbar, but the sandbar is also affected by the waves. This situation is never static, so one must constantly seek to understand the influence each is having on the other.

Analysis is never complete.

Guidelines for Newspaper Analysis

A. General
1. What does the title of the newspaper signify?
2. In the biggest headlines, what message is it trying to get across to the public?
3. The first page is trying to get a message to the public, what is it?
4. What is the message carried in the photographs? Who is in the pictures? How often?

B. Editorial
1. Is it the opinion of the newspaper?
   of the government?
   of the party?

C. Content Analysis
In analysing the content of a newspaper, there are two levels that need to be looked at: the official line of the government and items on independent and small local efforts not attached to government.

<u>1.</u> Development.
Official: What types of development are reported?
What is the economic orientation in the interviews, speeches, projects presented?
Grassroots: What and how much is reported on small local efforts?
What campaigns, strikes and independent actions are reported, and then how are they presented?

<u>2.</u> Politics.
Official: Who are the principal actors?
What are their speeches like?
What do they aim at?
What are their commitments to tribe or other factors?
Grassroots: What organisations at the grassroots are mentioned?
Who are the popular leaders?
What are their concerns?

<u>3.</u> Values.
Official: What are the most important key words used?
What are the most important themes and in whose favour are they?
What is presented as culture?
What is the place given to religion?
What is the place given to security?
What is valued more, property or human life?
Grassroots: Is expression of the common person given in the press? How?

D. International Information.
From what sources is international information received? (AP, UP are from USA, Reuter — Britain.)
How much international news is of:
Africa, Third World countries, Europe, USA, and Eastern countries.

What are the major themes from the international news?
Of which countries does the paper give favourable accounts, and of which countries does it give unfavourable accounts?

3.   Newspaper Analysis

The guidelines on the previous page can help people understand how newspapers form opinions of the public. Before the workshop, collect copies of the different newspapers published and most widely read. Take them to the workshop. Ask people to work in pairs.

In a serious study group, all questions could be answered. In a workshop, this outline can be given to the group, but ask the group to work only on two sections, perhaps Section C.1. on Development and item A. which is a general way of knowing roughly what emphasis is put into newspapers.

4.   The Newspaper Perspective Exercise*

This simple exercise helps people to become critical of the viewpoint from which articles in different newspapers or radio news, is written.

Procedure

1. As a group make a list of all the newspapers or radio stations which people know, and add others likely to present a strong point of view, e.g. from some particular foreign countries.
2. Divide into small groups of 2 – 4 people. Read a very short factual account of an imaginary news item which might be interpreted in very different ways by different newspapers depending on the origin and the interests of those who control the paper or radio. (For example, the end of an unsuccessful strike, the announcement of a large grant for military aid to a particular country, the protest of a group of doctors about a new system of free health care, the successful air attack on a guerilla training camp, etc.)
3. Ask each group to write a news report or article **from the particular point of view** of the newspaper their small group is to represent. Ask each group to read their report to the whole group.

Analyse the different versions on:

Language	Heroes/Villains	Omissions/Additions
(emotional words like terrorist or freedom fighter)	(who are presented as the victims and who are presented as the oppressors)	(what changes are made in the original news item to exaggerate or make a point)

Discuss whether the range of emphasis is really typical of newspaper or radio reports or not. What are the implications of this for the ordinary person? How is this done in our own country? What are the alternatives for gaining other sources of information?

---

* This exercise was originally designed by Sr. Janice McLaughlin (now with ZIMFEP, Harare, Zimbabwe) and Jane Vella.

5.   **Guidelines for Political Analysis**

The following 2 sets of questionnaires are linked to the economic analysis explained earlier in this chapter. We present a short and a longer one and their use depends on the aim of your group.

Simple Political Schema

1.   Begin by brainstorming with a group. **What do you see happening**:
— in the field of politics
— on the local level,
— on the national level.
Write a preliminary statement expressing your major insights on the political situation.
Now it is necessary to verify whether your understanding of the situation is accurate. These questions might be useful in doing so.

2.   a.   What are the most important **groups, organisations and classes** involved in the events you have mentioned?
b.   Use the Dynamic Model and identify the institutions operating at the national level on the side of the Dominant classes.
— How do these institutions operate at local level?
— Are there other organisations operating in the political field at local level? If yes, who?
c.   What are the institutions among the Oppressed Classes which try to build alternative types of organisations? Give examples.
— Do they inter-relate or do they oppose each other? On what basis?

3.   Choose the most important political **event** during the last year
— at local level,
— at national level.
a.   initiated by the Dominant classes,
b.   initiated by the Oppressed classes.
— Why do you think this event was so important?
— How did each group react to the event?
— How was this event reported in different newspapers? (Make a collection of newspaper cuttings and paste them up for people to see.)
— What were the strong feelings of different types of people in this event?

More Detailed Political Schema

For groups who would like to study more in depth, the following questions can be helpful, along with the above questionnaire.

1. List the political parties in the area.
   a. What social/economic forces does each party represent?
   b. Determine the approximate proportion of each social class in each party.
   c. How is each local party linked to the:
      — national party?
      — national economic forces?
      — international financial structures?

2. List the major Labour Unions in the area. Any union, group, movement has a political tendency. For our purposes here, we can categorise as follows:

On Right	Middle	On Left
(status quo or backwards)	(promote a few reforms)	(structural change, anti-capitalist in theory and action)

3. For each major labour union:
   a. What are their aims,
   b. what are their tendencies (right, middle, left)
   c. what are their preoccupations,
   d. what are their own limitations as a group (e.g. internal conflicts, disorganisation, no base, etc.)
   e. what are their strengths,
   f. what is their impact on their own class,
   g. what is their impact within the situation,
   h. what are their links to political parties,
   i. what are their links to local, national and international corporations?

4. List other groups, associations, religious groups, movements or organisations among the auxiliary and oppressed classes. For each group, answer all the above questions under number 3, but add the question of the links of this group with trade unions.

5. List the groups, associations, movements or organisations of 'intellectuals' which relate to grassroot groups. Again, answer all the questions found in number 3.

6. Are there any United Fronts in your area?
   a. What are their aims? Short term — long term.
   b. What is their platform?
   c. Their limitations and strengths.
   d. Who is the United Front aiming at involving?
   e. Against whom is the United Front directed?

7. What is the nature of political leadership in the area?
   a. What is the record of members of parliament?
      Who are their major supporters?
      Their previous occupation, social class, religion?
   b. What is the record of county and city councillors from your area?
      Who are their major supporters?
      Their previous occupation, social class, religion?
   c. What is the record of local officials?
      Who are their major supporters?
      Their previous occupation, social class, religion?

8. a. List 5 laws (national or local) which are important **obstacles** to the people?
   b. List 5 laws which promote/protect the oppressed class which could be the bases of change.

9. Give examples of one law that favours, or makes life harder for one or the other of each of the following groups:
   landlords/tenants
   Whites/Blacks
   African/Asian
   Men/Women
   Employers/Employees
   Urban Dwellers/Rural Dwellers.

F. Values and Beliefs

Both motivation to struggle for change, and apathy, are profoundly affected by the beliefs and values, myths and symbols through which people affirm their identity, explain what they want to live for, and hold out elements of hope.

Any group attempting to build a movement for change needs to understand the Group Psychology of the communities with which they are working, in order to find binding and energising symbols. They also need to recognise which beliefs undermine the people's confidence in their ability to bring about change.

It is exciting to **brainstorm** with a group, **examples of how a symbol,** a dream, a myth, a gesture **has inspired** people to extraordinary commitment at different times in different countries.

Gandhi's dream of the ocean breakers crashing on the rocks and the sea salt, God's free gift, crystallising in the sun, inspired him to start the Great Salt March. Thousands of people joined him to protest the British Tax on Salt in India. This symbolic gesture raised awareness of colonial oppression throughout the country.

In the struggle for Independence in Zimbabwe, the spirit medium, Mbuya Nehanda, who had led the resistance in the 'first Chimurenga' in 1896, proved a great inspiration to the freedom fighters in the late 1970's.

The following guideline helps us to look at Group Psychology.

1.   Group Psychology Questionnaire

1. Describe the Dominant Ideology (the values, beliefs, myths). Brainstorm a list — categorise them — elaborate on them.
    — Which of these values, beliefs, myths has a historical basis which could build towards a more social-communal future?

2. Describe the alternative ideologies being presented in your area.

3. What institutions or groups are expressing, reproducing or disseminating the:
    a. Dominant Ideology, (be precise)
    b. The Alternative Ideologies.
4. What social classes are related to each.

5. How does each:
    a. explain what people want to live for,
    b. explain the social and historical reasons for daily events,
    c. hold out elements of hope,
    d. affirm an identity.

6. As more conflicts/tensions emerge from the economic crisis of capitalism, how are economic and social issues explained by the Dominant classes,.and the tensions relieved, by means of:
    a. symbols,
    b. traditions,
    c. slogans,
    d. symbolic gestures,
    e. calling upon mythical historical events,
    f. other.
    How do Alternative Ideologies explain the above (6 a – d)? How do they build on old symbols, traditions, myths or develop new ones?

7. Paulo Freire said that it is not so much the pitiful situation of the masses which saddens him, but their capacity to accept the situation.
    — What hinders or stops the peoples' will to act for or against something?
    — What are the historical, cultural, religious or ideological factors which explain this more or less passive acceptance?
    — What are the forces working to domesticate or repress people?

Proverbs are the daughters of experience.
— Burundi proverb

2.   RELIGION

Fr. Joseph Donders, the professor of religion and philosophy at the University of Nairobi once said:

"There can be good religion,
bad religion, and
very bad religion."

The Bible shows us throughout the Old Testament that the call of God is a call to 'do justice', to set right what is wrong. The prophets challenged the people again and again to do justice towards the poor. When Jesus announced his mission in the synagogue at Nazareth he said,

"He has sent me to bring good news to the poor,
to proclaim liberty to captives
and to the blind new sight,
to set the downtrodden free,
to proclaim the Lord's year of favour."

Later he said, "I have come that you may have life and have it to the full."

There is no doubt that the message of Christianity calls us to complete commitment to the struggle for a world where every person will have the opportunity for full human development, challenging and turning upside down the values of our greedy modern world.

The message of the Gospel is Radical, affirming some of the values of every culture and turning other values upside down. But all religions have to set up institutions to spread their message. As the institutions grow they easily become preoccupied with their own preservation. They become weighed down with property, with history, and very often for the sake of stability, the Institution grows conservative and supports the status quo — supports those in power even if they are clearly unjust.

It is important to analyse what role each religion is playing in the struggle for a just society, or in blocking the process of liberation and transformation. The following questionnaire will help us to look critically at the role the different religions are playing in our society.

a.   Religion Questionnaire

1. List the principal religions in the area.
2. Approximately how many people in each?
3. Approximately, what percentage of social classes are their believers?
4. What groups affirm the values, beliefs of the Dominant class?
5. What groups criticise it?
6. What values, beliefs, support the Dominant class?
7. What values, beliefs, denounce aspects of the status quo and announce an alternative?
8. What is the most important sphere of influence of each religious group?
9. What is the most important social impact of each religious group?

b.   **Different Levels of Awareness among Christians**

The following is one way of explaining the growth of awareness
from concern for the poor
to community transformation.

1. The **Gospel challenges us to Charity** towards the Poor.
2. Acts of charity **challenge us to Analysis,** "What are the causes of poverty?"
3. Analysis **challenges us to join the Struggle** of the poor, of particular groups, e.g. landless, workers, peasants.
4. Participation in the struggle **challenges us to re-think the** Gospel and to challenge the Institution.

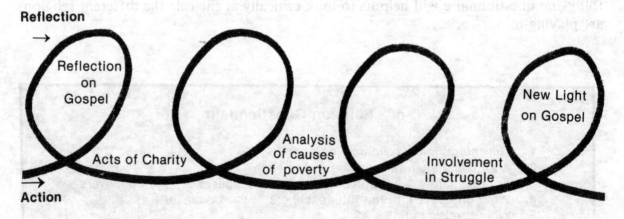

Discussion Questions

1. To what extent does the Institutional Church in your situation serve the message?
2. To what extent does it submerge the message?

c. **Religious Institutions Analysis**

It is very useful to use the 3 Storey Building as·a framework for analysing the situation of the Church in a diocese or country.

Procedure
1. Ask groups of 4 or 5's first to list the relevant questions in each section: Economic, Political and Ideological.
2. Share these questions in the whole group and choose those that are most relevant.
3. Return to groups to find out the answers to each question. This can be done first on the basis of sharing perceptions. Later these should be checked through research.
4. What helps and what hinders the Church's contribution to the process of justice?
5. What do **we** need to do about this?

Summary

In the Exodus, God calls His People out of Slavery, to journey towards the Promised Land. He tells Moses,

"I have seen the misery of my People,
I have heard their cry to be free
    of their slave drivers.
Yes, I am well aware of their sufferings.
I mean to deliver them
    out of the hands of their oppressors
and bring them to a land rich and broad —
    a land flowing with milk and honey."

But after some years, **the Promised Land has itself become a Land of Slavery**. People are enslaved again in a different way. There is a need for a new exodus.

The people are forced to go into exile.
This happens again and again in history.
In what way do the people in our country need liberation?

> "The people must preside over the process of historical transformation now taking place in Zimbabwe. The era where people were regarded as the objects of the civilising mission of the Church must give way to the advent of people as subjects of their own destiny. As people recover their own identity . . . they dream their own historical vision. This is the sacred process of self-determination, selfhood and self-reliance. . . . The Church ought to discover the wisdom and genius of the people from the roots of their own history of the struggles to be human. . . .
>
> If the Church can appreciate the dynamics of the new social order it can adequately perform the task of watchdog in ensuring regard for the human factor in the process of development. The Church should embark on a research and analysis of the type of development that seeks a perfect expression of human values."
>
> Canaan Banana
> **The Gospel According to the Ghetto**
> p. 96.

d.   **Vision of the Church. An Exercise.**

This exercise is very helpful with parish or diocesan groups.

Procedure

1.   Ask people to divide into groups of 5. These can **either** be groups from similar vocations (e.g. all priests, sisters, catechists, lay men, lay women). This highlights the different perspective of different groups in the final sharing. If one group usually tends to be very quiet, this can ensure their voice is really heard.

Or the groups can be as mixed as possible. This means the exchange between people takes place in the small groups.

It is best for each group to sit around a separate table.

2.   Give a few minutes for each person to think about the Church as they have actually experienced it. They can jot down a few notes or draw a few images.

3   Ask each group to share their ideas and then make a drawing of the Church **as they have experienced it**.

4.   When they have done this, ask them to think individually for a short while, and then make a second communal drawing of the Church **as you long for it to be**.

5.   When the drawings are completed, ask each group to stick their two pictures up side by side on the wall and have a Gallery Walk, giving everyone an opportunity to see all the posters and ask questions of the other groups.

6.   In the whole group **discuss the questions:**

a.   What are the most striking similarities and the most striking differences in the posters?

b.   What are the implications of this for me? For us as a group?

Allow a short time of quiet silent reflection, perhaps an opportunity to walk outside, before sharing this last question.

e.   **Models of the Church***

This input can be given on its own as the basis of discussion, or used after the previous exercise, after a short break.

The church can be seen in each of the following ways:

1.   **Institution of Salvation**

	Motto	'You are Peter, and on this rock. . .'
	Present	In the traditional Catholic model, including Vatican II, Lumen Gentium chapter 3.
	Emphasis	Church as a means of salvation, stressing death and life after death. Clarity of pronouncements on faith and morals. Sense of separation from and/or superiority to the world. 'Outside the church there is no salvation.'
	Politics	Church itself is a political power. Concordats. Influence on politics through Christian parties.
	Workers	Emphasis on Christian morality. If possible Christian unions, strongly anti-communist.

* Avery Dulles, *Models of the Church*, Gill and Macmillan, London, 1976.

2.   **Mystical Communion**

Motto	'Where two or three are gathered together in my name, there am I in the midst of you.'
Present	In charismatic and pentecostal groups. Vatican II. Church as body of Christ, and as people of God.
Emphasis	Openness to the Spirit. Concern for each individual.
Politics	Seen as a worldly and dirty affair. The Church has a spiritual mission and must not interfere. The State guarantees law, order and tranquillity and is God's instrument.
Workers	Organised into prayer groups. Denial of class conflict.

3.   **Herald**

Motto	'Go out into the whole world and proclaim. . . .'
Present	In Lutheran and other reformed protestant churches, missionary congregations.
Emphasis	Prophetic role, denouncing evil and announcing the good news.
Politics	Theory of two kingdoms. Politics is the domain of the rulers, but God is in control.
Workers	Bible groups. Pronouncements on the rights of workers.

4.   **Sacrament**

Motto	'You are the light of the world.'
Present	In Vatican II. Most of 'Lumen Gentium'.
Emphasis	God is at work in the world and dialogue with others is important. The church as a visible sign of God's grace, a sign of hope of the new society modelled on the values of the kingdom.
Politics	Church should play a prophetic role through what she is and what she says and does. Distinguishes between party politics and social injustice. It shows that an alternative type of society is possible through example of religious communities.
Workers	Recognises the autonomy of the unions and supports them. Seen as domain of laity.

5.   Servant of the Kingdom

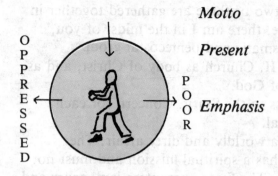

Motto   'Let us go outside the camp and share his degradation'. Heb. 13:13.

Present   In Medellin. Some basic Christian communities. Wherever the church has taken an option for the poor.

Emphasis   The problem is not does God exist, but do human beings exist? Through involvement with the poor we come to understand God, and Jesus the 'poor servant'. Creation is good. Incarnation taken seriously.

Politics   A people's church, from below, taking sides with the poor and the oppressed. Ready to die as an institution and forget her own interests. In opposition to oppressive states.

Workers   Identifying with the cause of the workers and ready to pay the price.

"Is not this the fast that pleases me
to break unjust fetters
and undo the thongs of the yoke,
to let the oppressed go free
and break every yoke
to share your bread with the hungry
and shelter the homeless poor."

Isaiah 58:6 – 12

Socialism and Christianity

"I am sure that many members of the clergy are revulsed at the thought that our brand of socialism is one based on Marxist-Leninist principles for they cannot forget that Marx said of religion that it was the opium of the masses. Whatever his own religious views might have been, and he was free to express them, I wish to stand firm on the assertion that the morality of socialism in terms of its principles and objectives to the people is far higher than the morality of capitalism, if capitalism has any morality at all. Indeed the issues can be reduced to one of conflict between morality and immorality.

As we have repeatedly held, ZANU does not see any contradiction between socialism and Christianity. Indeed we would expect that greater and quicker response to our socialist call would be forthcoming from those who profess Christianity than from the non-Christian circles. I admit that the earlier practice of socialism in some countries led to the near extinction of Christianity in those countries, but that was also because Christianity in those countries had stood for the old order and had resisted the new social order. In socialist countries like Poland and Bulgaria Christianity has been allowed to develop unabated in the transformative process from capitalism to communism.

If Christianity's main criticism of socialism or communism is that it is too much of materialism and very little of God, my retort is: Give it a God, the God of socialism, but please, never the God of capitalism. In my view, true Christianity should feel more at home in a socialist environment than in a capitalist one."

Prime Minister **Robert Mugabe**
from a speech to the Catholic Justice and Peace Commission, February, 1982.

3. FIVE RESPONSES TO POVERTY

It is important for any group attempting to help the poor, to be clear what kind of service they are offering. The way we analyse the causes of the problem affects our goals, and the kind of program we develop. (A group using the Parabola Model found in Chapter 10, may find that the different levels of doubt amongst members are closely linked to different analysis of causes of the problem and therefore different priorities in goals.)

On the next pages, we include **two different models, linking analysis of causes with different goals**. A group should see which of these two models is most appropriate for use in their own situation.

FIVE RESPONSES TO POVERTY		
	1	**2**
A. Causes of the Problem	Circumstances beyond the control of Local people. Natural Disasters Bad Luck	Lack of Education Lack of Resources causing low standard of living
B. Goals	To Relieve Suffering	To Raise Production To Subdue Nature
C. Service programs	Famine Relief Refugee Centres Care of Disabled Child Care Clinics	Technical Training in agriculture, home industries, income producing activities, health care, savings and credit
D. Type of Change Involved	FUNCTIONAL CHANGE ←——————————————————————→ Non-Conflictual Models	
E. Type of Leadership	Strong Reliance on Authority	Consultative
F. Inspiration	Charity. Help the Poor.	Help People to Help Themselves. Vatican II.
G. Type of Service	WELFARE	DEVELOPMENT

FIVE RESPONSES TO POVERTY

3	4	5
Poor Functioning of Structures, Education, Health, Agriculture Services	Exploitation Domination Oppression	Inadequate Structures
To make existing structures work more fairly.	To Challenge and Overcome Exploitative Structures	To build new economic, political, legal and education structures.
Supplementary Services, e.g. Extra classes, Legal Aid, Citizen's Advice Bureaus Organise to reform structures	Trade Unions, Political Parties and movements Conscientization Programs	Conscientization Programs Alternative Structures, co-ops, workers councils, New forms of Education
⟶	STRUCTURAL CHANGE ⟷ Conflictual Models	
Participatory Shared Responsibility	Shared but Delegation of Authority from base up. Strong Discipline.	Animation. Enabling. Participatory. Shared Responsibility.
Equal Rights Equal Opportunities Vatican II	Liberation Theology Denouncing Evil Announcing Good.	'Behold I make all Things New.'
LIBERAL REFORMATION	LIBERATION	TRANSFORMATION

Level	FOUR LEVELS OF AWARENESS The Community Situation. Typical Attitudes-Actions	
Closed or Broken Consciousness — Naive — Dependent — Alienated — Suppressed	Closed Societies, not open to change, **or** Broken Societies, where new patterns seem impossible to understand. Culture of Silence. Fatalism or Resignation. 'It must be the Will of God.' 'The way things are is the only way they can ever be.' Magical explanation for happenings, e.g. curses, bewitching. Nature, Culture and History **are given to us**, not shaped by us. Unquestioning acceptance of explanations of those in power, 'that the rich deserve to be rich and poor are lazy and ignorant'. Unchanging repetition of activities to meet basic needs, traditional rituals, celebrating great deeds of the past but little effort to change present or future.	
Awakening Consciousness — Alert — Rebellious — Critical of people and events but not questioning established system.	Signs of limited change, e.g. technology, buildings, social patterns. Conflicts developing between groups with different interests. Awareness of inequality, injustice, not sharing, 'the fruits of independence', but dealing with symptoms, not root causes. Attempts to reorganise some elements of economic, social and cultural life, e.g. demand for better wages, changed family relationships, great faith in more opportunities for formal schooling. Local actions to meet immediate needs. 'Harambee' or self-help projects.	
Reforming Consciousness — Start of struggle to improve functioning of the system.	Recognition of Different Classes with opposing interests. Open Conflicts. Beginning of Trade Unions, Farmers Associations, etc. Desire for Self-Determination, reliance on own reserves. Moving from perception to analysis. Starting to question, 'Why do the rich get richer while the poor get poorer?' 'Why do some have so much power?' A Struggle to share power in partnership with the ruling group. Still little questioning of pyramid structure of authority or of some ruling class values, e.g. laws that protect property more than people. Demands for higher wages, shorter hours. Use of slogans. Struggle for existing power positions, different faces at the top, not change of structures.	
Liberating and Transforming Consciousness	Development of new relationship between classes. — Deep questioning of old values and expression of new values. — Creative development of new types of structures expressing these values. Recognition that freedom is never achieved 'once and for all'. Therefore personal and group involvement is a permanent process of renewal and liberation, constantly guarding against new patterns of oppression.	

FOUR LEVELS OF AWARENESS	
Types of Assistance	
Approaches that Reinforce Present Situation	**Approaches which contribute to Transformation**
Paternalistic approaches — doing things for people. Responding to needs as emergencies. Free handouts. Building dependence. Offering opportunities for advance of individuals but not developing communal responsibility for whole community. Sharing life of the poor without getting involved with them in a struggle to transform the situation.	Identifying social and economic classes. Finding people and groups more aware, articulate, able to explain causes and influence others. Finding aspects of local religion and culture with liberating message. Enabling people to break the culture of silence, to speak openly and honestly, trusting their experience. Gain skills by forming and running organisations to meet local needs.
Prompt actions to satisfy immediate needs. Regrouping of the people around local leaders who 'take over' actions initiated by the community. Small community development projects with authoritarian leadership which do not train people in democratic participation and decision-making.	Enabling different groups to express their insights, expectations and reasons for action. Searching for causes of injustice. Developing new patterns of decision-making and small projects involving a process of joint planning, action/reflection/action, etc. Avoiding taking 'most aware' out of community, but channelling their insight and commitment into shared community responsibility.
Large organisations with centralised authoritarian patterns of work, which impose ideology on others not challenging them to think for themselves. Desire to share in economic growth but not questioning the type of growth. Recognition of only one type of valid action. Seeing politics primarily in terms of elections.	Models which help groups analyse situation critically and plan action. Pinpointing clashes of interests — between classes in society, — within the organisation. Constant dialogue between leaders and masses Action/Reflection cycle leading to constant evaluation of values, aims and strategies. Relate struggle to processes of history.
Over-emphasis on technology for the sake of efficiency. Allowing tribal, racial or cultural differences to divide those who basically share the same interests. Haphazard attacks on international imperialism rather than careful strategy.	Support constant struggle within the movement to reflect on personal and organisational life. Try creative new experiments. Get rid of authoritarian structures. Develop self-management and active participation at all levels. Keep open communication with grass roots. Building international solidarity and strong links with other groups involved in similar struggles.

59

4.   LEVELS OF CONSCIOUSNESS

Critical assessment of the levels of consciousness of the groups we are working with, and of our own type of assistance, helps to ensure that our work is really part of a process of transformation and is not merely reinforcing the existing situation.

Presentation of theory

1. A small group, who has studied carefully the chart on the foregoing pages, can prepare 4 short plays in which 4 different groups, each revealing how a different level of consciousness deals with the same problem. The problem must of course be relevant to the group concerned.

    For example, one could have 4 different conversations about the fact that a number of children in a particular area have died of dysentery. The first group would reveal all the attitudes of the first level of closed or broken consciousness. The second group the attitudes of awakening consciousness, etc.

2. After the plays, brainstorm and write on 4 separate sheets of newsprint the attitudes and actions of the people in each of the 4 plays. Use this as the basis for clarification of the 4 different levels of consciousness.

3. Ask each person or team to fill in answers to the questions below in regard to any one group with which they are working.

Analysis of Different Levels of Consciousness

a. What is the situation regarding change and stability, in the life situation of the group:
    — economic
    — social
    — political
    — cultural
b. What is the attitude of the people towards the problems, difficulties, sufferings, and changes in their lives?
    How do they attempt to explain them?
c. What types of action have they taken to try to improve their lives?

---

4. Hand out copies of the chart found on the previous pages, and ask the team to identify the level of consciousness of the group they were discussing, and then to evaluate critically their own type of assistance to the group in the light of points in the two columns on the right.

"Utopia is born in the springs of hope.
It is responsible for
models that seek a perfecting of our reality,
models which do not allow the social process
to stagnate, nor society to absolutize itself,
models that maintain society permanently
open to ever-increasing transformation."

Leonardo Boff
Jesus Christ Liberator, p. 45.

G. Vision of a New Society

The aim of this exercise is to help people think into the future in a creative and constructive way. So often we look for the root causes of problems in society and we can be critical. But in order to have a liberating and transforming consciousness, we all need to have a vision of the future. This vision must be concrete.

The following 12 different areas of life can be explored in 12 different groups. Groups should be at least 3 members but not more than 7. If a topic is not chosen then just leave it out.

Time 2 – 3 hours.

Materials Newsprint, markers, tape

Instructions and questions for each group.

Instructions

What kind of society do we want? Not an unreal society where all the problems have already been solved, but one that is realistically coping with the problems: not putting the clock back, or ignoring irreversible trends (such as urbanisation) but building on what is good, human and possible in the modern world. Use the following questions to clarify the kind of society you would like to live in, the kind of laws and institutions which would help to ensure a happy and satisfying life for **all** the inhabitants. If necessary adapt the questions to suit your own situation.

Each group should **draw up a list of 3 to 5 recommendations, and prepare a visual demonstration** (diagram, poster, model, short play or demonstration) illustrating why you offer a particular recommendation or how it might work.

1.   **Work in Agriculture**
   a. What are the laws on ownership and distribution of land?
   b. Who are the major producers in agriculture? Why? What changes are needed in their conditions, in order to increase their productivity?
   c. Should emphasis be on cash crops or food?
            small or large farms?
            individual small holdings, co-operative, or collective farming?
   d. Is it important that rural people live in villages?
   e. What kinds of tools and technology would be most helpful?
   f. What kind of organisations do farmers and agricultural workers need?
   g. What should be the priorities in the budget for the department of agriculture?

2.   **Work in Industry**
   a. What type and structure of industry is there? Why? How can it be changed?
   b. Who should decide what is produced and how should it be decided?
   c. Who should own the factories, processing plants, etc.?
       Who should determine the conditions of production?
   d. In what way should the workers participate
            — in sharing the profits?
            — in ownership of the factory?
            — in decision-making?

   e. Should profits be shared — within each industry?
                           — between different industries?
   f. What are the advantages and disadvantages of state ownership?
   g. What needs to be done to prevent a few people exploiting others?
   h. What is the relationship between industry and the life of the community as a whole?

3.   **Health**
   a. How could you develop a good balance between promotion of health, prevention of disease and curative medicine?
   b. Do you agree that the good health of the community depends more on pure water supply, latrines, balanced diet, and adequate income, than on medical services? If so what are the implications?
   c. What can be done to encourage community responsibility for health?

d. What could be done to overcome the problem that nearly all trained medical personnel (doctors and nurses) want to work in big hospitals, towns or cities and that the rural areas get neglected?

e. What kind of health workers do we need to train to bring basic health education and services within reach of every village?

f. How could we make sure that most of those given the opportunity to do nursing or medical training are committed to serve the needs of people rather than to getting prestige and money for themselves?

g. What could be done to prevent the illegal sale of medicines for private profit?

4.   **Housing (urban)**

a. What could be done to provide adequate housing in rapidly growing cities?

b. Should low cost housing be owned and subsidised by the city or town council?

c. Should there be rent control? Should rent be a fixed percentage of income?

d. As nearly all housing projects built by city councils turn out to be too expensive for the poor, would it be better to provide 'site and service' schemes? (i.e. where people get a plot, roads, water, sewerage, and electricity etc., but have to build their own houses). What help would people need? How could this be organised?

e. What about ownership? Should people be allowed to own their own houses? Just one house? Or as many as they want to?

5.   **Money — Wages, Credit, Foreign Investment, etc.**

a. Should there be minimum wages?

b. Should there be any kind of control limiting the amount of money one person can make?

c. What range should there be between minimum and maximum incomes?

d. Is there any way to ensure adequate incomes for subsistence farmers? Or is it more important to ensure that essential services such as education, medical services are free and available to all?

e. How could we ensure that everybody has the opportunity to save money, and to borrow money for worthwhile purposes?

f. Is it possible in rural areas to work towards an 'interdependent community' where there is work for all as people produce and sell the goods needed by their neighbours, and buy the goods made by their neighbours?

g. What effect does the present system of imports and exports have on employment? How does the import and export policy affect the rich? the poor?

h. What really needs to be imported for the overall development of the country?

i. Who produces most of the goods exported? Do they benefit from the foreign exchange earned by these exports? Is there too much emphasis on cash crops for export and the importing of luxury goods?

j. What are the advantages and disadvantages of encouraging tourism? Does it bring much benefit to the ordinary people? Who does benefit?

k. What are the advantages and disadvantages of encouraging foreign investment?

6. **Education (Children)**

   a. Should primary education be free? compulsory?
   b. Should there be exams?
   c. What changes need to be made in primary schools to prepare people to contribute to genuine development, get away from 'certificate fever' and 'white collar ambitions'? What changes in subjects taught? What changes in general organisation of the schools?
   d. What can be done to develop initiative, creativity, responsibility and communal concern in the children?
   e. Should there be changes in secondary education?
      How should selection to secondary schools be made?
   f. What arrangements should be made for technical training? Are village polytechnics (trade schools) a satisfactory solution? Could an effective system of apprenticeship be worked out? or Workers' Brigades? What could be done to develop managerial skills, so that people with technical training, e.g. building and masonry can organise their own work and not depend on 'ready-made jobs'?

7. **Specialised Training and Higher Education**

   a. What kind of specialised training should be given priority, (e.g. teacher training; adult educators, etc.).
   b. How should candidates be selected?
   c. How should university students be selected?
   d. Should students be given grants or loans to pay for their fees?
   e. Should graduates be better paid than other workers?
   f. How can the work of the university be related much more closely to the needs of the community?

8. **Adult Education**

   a. Should adult education be a priority? Why? How should a system of basic education for all be organised?
   b. What should it include?
   c. How can adult education be linked to development, human and communal?
      — in production, in agriculture
      — in social and political organisation
      — in health care, etc.?
   d. How should religious education for adults be organised? What should it be focused on? Who should do it? How should the educators be trained?
   e. Should adult education programmes also deal with cultural values? In what way?

9. **Family Relationships**

   a. What type of family relationships and loyalties would we like to see in the future?
   b. Is the 'nuclear family unit' (father, mother and children) the ideal model?
   c. How can we retain what is good in the African concept of extended family?
   d. How can we deal with the pressures put upon the family (both nuclear and extended) by modern life, urbanisation, migrant labour etc.?
   e. In what ways are role expectations of women and of men changing? Can anything be done to encourage the positive changes and discourage the negative ones?

f. What needs to be done to help make marriage a satisfying relationship for both men and women?

g. What could be done to encourage communication between different generations? In a rapidly changing society how can we help to make the 'gap' in outlook a less painful experience?

h. What could be done to help make old age a happy time?

10. Political Participation

a. What do you consider priorities of good government? Is it important for as many people as possible to be genuinely involved in decision-making? If so why?

b. If participation is important how can it be organised effectively
    — at local level (village or town)
    — at district and provincial level
    — at national level?

c. Is political education necessary? If so how can it be done effectively?

d. What types of barazas (community meetings), decision-making procedures etc. would be helpful?

e. What can be done to make sure that political leaders remain accountable to the people they represent?

f. What could be done to prevent — individuals or groups entrenching themselves in power and refusing to give it up?
    — corruption
    — other abuse of power?

g. What could be done to make sure that government policy is effectively carried out by government officials who are capable, honest and have a spirit of service to the public?

11. Religion

a. What role would we like to see the Churches playing in society?

b. What structures would be needed to encourage communication between
    — people in different roles within one church
    — people of different religions

c. What human needs are being met by traditional religions and independent Churches — and what changes could be brought about in the Catholic (or other mainline) Church to meet these needs more fully?

d. What changes are needed — in liturgy
    Why?   — in community life? (e.g. to encourage Basic Christian Communities)

e. In what ways can religion enrich the whole quality of life for people, and what can we do to see that it fulfils this role wherever possible.

f. Does preaching and teaching today give most Christians deep trust in a loving God, concern for one another and hope for the future?

12. **Recreation & Cultural Values**

a. What aspects of traditional African culture and custom do we value and wish to keep? Which aspects do we feel are negative and should be changed?

b. Which Western values (or values of the scientific technological society) do we value and wish to keep?

c. How could people be helped to make choices about cultural values in life? In what way could this be done in adult education programmes?

d. What could be done by governments, Church and other voluntary groups, to foster values which lead to the happiness of the whole community and discourage negative attitudes?

e. In what ways could creative expression in art, music, dance, drama and other forms be encouraged?

f. What could be done to make life interesting and enjoyable for all (old and young, men and women) in rural areas? — in urban areas?

g. What were the high points of celebration of life, joy, community, in traditional society? Should anything be done to retain or adapt these in modern life?

h. What new forms of recreational facilities need to be provided in rural and urban areas?

i. Is it important to encourage active rather than passive recreation? How?

H. Guidelines for Building a Just Society

Father Donal Dorr (Kiltegan), has given 10 points as guidelines for building a just society. A list of these points can be given to a group. In small groups, people can discuss whether they agree or disagree with these points and what other elements they would add to the list.

1. Redistribute **goods**.
   Meet basic needs first, giving priority to the poorest.
2. Redistribute **power**.
3. Change the structures, not just the rulers.
4. Build structures for **participation** and a tradition of participation.
5. Do not confuse a great leader with good structures. The test is: Do the improvements continue after the leader has left?
6. A change of structures and a change of attitudes are both needed.
7. Motivation of envy, hate and greed is self-defeating.
8. Do not sacrifice a generation now, to build the future.
9. The **means** chosen affect the **end**. In fact, the means add up to the form the end.
10. So, **live** the **future** you hope for, **now**. The future is a set of embodied values.

Chapter 10

Building a Movement

This chapter includes:

Chapter 10

Building a Movement*

Any group committed to transformation, either through fostering Basic Christian Communities which are working for development and social justice, or through a party or political movement, needs to build supportive structures and patterns of working with people that are consistent with their overall aims.

A human, caring and supportive structure is necessary to maintain the commitment of people, to challenge them, and enable them to fulfil their role in the organisation or movement as effectively as possible. All of us are human beings and we all have limitations and faults. The structures we make should enable individuals and groups to develop their strengths and give them the necessary encouragement and affirmation. They should also reduce the negative consequences of personal limitations and faults, building a system of accountability, and providing regular possibilities for constructive feedback to deal with the anxiety and frustration, which inevitably arise from time to time, within and between persons.

Organisational development helps to promote creative, enabling leadership and good co-ordination.

Leadership is an exercise of power. Many Christians have mixed feelings about power, because it is so often abused. But power in itself is good. It is an attribute of God Himself. After His Resurrection Jesus said, "all power is given to me in heaven and on earth" and after the "Our Father" we pray "For Thine is the Kingdom, the Power and the Glory". In so far as we are made in the Image of God, we share in His power, and we are called upon to co-create the world, making it a happy home for all its people. The responsible use of power is one of the most important moral and ethical issues of our time. In building good supportive structures we help to ensure that the power of each individual and the group as a whole is used for the good of all people.

* This chapter is based on the book, *Leadership: The Responsible Exercise of Power*. MDI Group, 110 East 8th Street, Cincinnati, Ohio 45202, USA, 1972. The MDI Group has had years of experience working with Protestant and Catholic dioceses, religious groups and educational and health institutions. We find their material extremely helpful for this next step of developing commitment through enabling structures. Permission to quote and adapt their materials has been given to the authors of this book.

> Any group working together needs clarity on three
> crucial points:
>   A.   **Goals**
>   B.   **Roles**
>   C.   **Relationships.**

Almost always when groups are having problems with 'communication' and 'co-operation' the source of the problem can be traced to lack of clarity or agreement in one of these areas. In building a movement and working in teams, it is essential to deal thoroughly with each of these areas.

A.   Goals

1.   THE PARABOLA

The Parabola is a very useful model for a group that already feels a certain common commitment, e.g. a literacy program, a parish, a development committee or a diocese. It stresses the importance of common vision and values, and clear goals. It can be used either to draw a group together to unite their efforts in planning new initiatives, or to evaluate past efforts, whether they were successful or not.

> It gives a group some important criteria for building
> commitment, and a very reliable framework, which helps them
> to proceed step by step together.

Sometimes it is best for the group to work on common perceptions of the needs of people first, using for example the exercise on 'Shape of the World' found on page 15, Book 3. Then the parabola needs to be used, fairly early in a workshop or program, to allow the participants plenty of time to work on each step.

Procedure

The model should be explained clearly drawing the parabola on a blackboard or on double sheets of newsprint. Each step in the development and the decline should be labelled.

Afterwards a copy of the model can be handed out to each participant. There should be an opportunity to ask questions, and then in small groups the participants can reflect on the model, applying it to a common experience if possible.

It is very helpful to ask them to draw curves for each project they are all familiar with (e.g. a literacy program, a youth club, a parish council) identifying what stage the project has now reached; which steps were done thoroughly, which inadequately. This helps them to pinpoint particular problems, and see clearly what needs to be done to strengthen a program.

Note: Linking the model to their own experience in this way enables them to internalise it and prepares them to use it as the basis for wider planning.

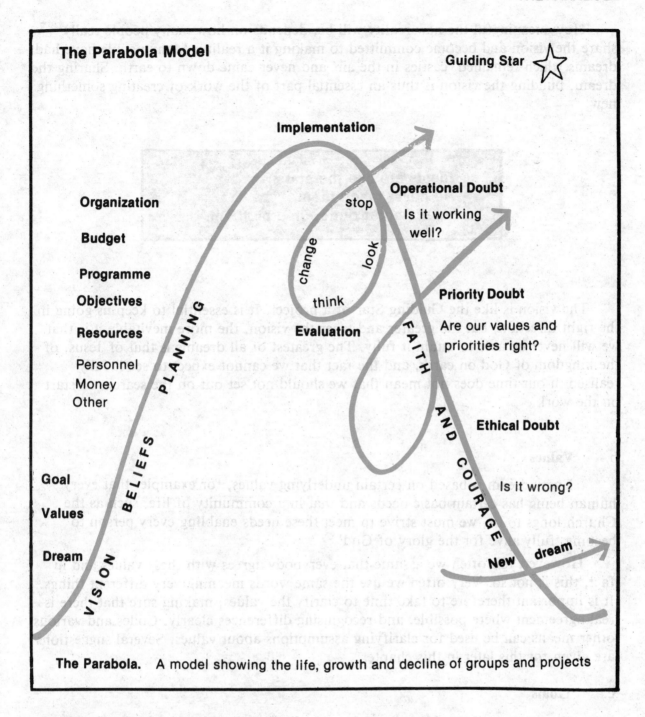

The Parabola Model

Guiding Star ☆

Implementation

Organization

Budget

Programme

Objectives

Resources

Personnel
Money
Other

PLANNING

BELIEFS

VISION

Goal

Values

Dream

stop

change   look

think

Evaluation

FAITH AND COURAGE

Operational Doubt

Is it working
well?

Priority Doubt

Are our values and
priorities right?

Ethical Doubt

Is it wrong?

New   dream

The Parabola.   A model showing the life, growth and decline of groups and projects

The Parabola Model Theory

A parabola is a geometrical shape, used often in graphs. It is a model that can enable us to understand the life, growth and decline of groups. It can be used for groups of all kinds and sizes from a simple youth club, to a social movement or a diocese.

a.   A Dream

Every new thing begins as a dream. Someone, somewhere, begins to see a new possibility. They start to share this dream or vision with others. Maybe there are some dreams which one person can carry out alone (e.g. making a work of art), but if this dream has anything to do with building a certain type of community (such as a home for the blind, a social movement, a diocese, a church, a political party), the dream will only become a reality to the extent that those who first think of it are able to share their vision with others.

How meaningful the new reality will be, depends on how many people really share the vision and become committed to making it a reality. Many people have had dreams which remained 'castles in the air' and never came down to earth. Sharing the dream, building the vision is thus an essential part of the work of creating something new.

> 'Ideals are like the stars.
> We never reach them,
> but we chart our course by them.'

The vision is like the Guiding Star of a project. It is essential to keep us going in the right direction, but the greater and truer the vision, the more inevitable it is that we will never be able to attain it fully. The greatest of all dreams is that of Jesus, of the kingdom of God on earth, and the fact that we cannot expect to see it fully realised in our time does not mean that we should not set out on the search, or start on the work.

b. Values

Every dream is based on certain underlying values, for example; that every human being has certain basic needs and that in a community of life, such as the Church longs to be, we must strive to meet these needs enabling every person to become 'fully alive for the glory of God'.

However, too often we assume that everybody agrees with these values and in fact, this is not so. Very often we use the same words meaning very different things. It is important therefore to take time to clarify the values, making sure that there is real agreement where possible, and recognising differences clearly. Codes and various other means can be used for clarifying assumptions about values. Several suggestions are given for this later in this chapter.

c. Goals

The next step in making the vision a reality is to set clear goals. To do this we need to decide on a certain date, sometime ahead like three years, and agree upon the situation we hope to have reached by that time. For example we might say, 'By the end of 1984 we hope to have well run and highly productive co-operatives in X number of places.' Another example could be, 'By the end of 1984 we hope to have active basic Christian communities in every out-station, caring for one another and reaching out to respond to the needs of their other neighbours; and we hope to have a trained team of animators in each parish.'

d. Resources

Next we need to consider the resources available and those which are needed in order to reach our goals. Without a doubt, far and away the most important resource is **committed and trained people**. How many of these are available will depend partly on how effectively we have shared the vision and the values,

As the project grows, the search for and the on-going training of such people must continue. In an organisation, the personnel may consist of full-time paid workers, but in a movement, the **voluntary workers will be as important if not more so than the full-time workers.** And we should realize that all the most important changes in history have come about through voluntary work, not primarily through efforts of those who were doing a job because they were being paid to do it.

We should also realise that though individuals are extremely important, the effectiveness of each one is multiplied many times if they are part of a strong supportive team and this is where the importance of team building and developing a movement, of clarity about roles, and work on good affirmative relationships comes in.

Far less important, but nevertheless necessary, are the other resources, which include:

— money,
— materials,
— equipment, and
— buildings.

Any project that is more concerned about money and material equipment than about personnel, is not likely to have much success.

e.   Objectives

On the basis of the personnel, and other resources available, the group now needs to set definite objectives. This means deciding precisely **what** one is going to do to reach the goal. (e.g. 'We will do a survey of the existing co-operatives, trying to identify what factors are contributing to their strength or weakness'. Or 'we will visit all the parishes asking them to select leaders in whom they have confidence and we will organise a series of four workshops to give these leaders more training.')

f.   Program

The next step is to decide **how** we are going to carry out our objectives. Many projects flop, though their objectives are good, because their program planning is bad. Program planning requires a deep understanding of the community as well as clear goals and objectives. The problem-posing method is very useful at this stage.

g.   Budget

A budget reflects clearly the priorities of the group. It is quite true to say, 'Show me how you spend your time and money, and I will know what your values are.' It is therefore very important to decide who should be involved, and in what way, in the process of drawing up the budget.

h.   Organisation

This step involves more detailed work on roles and includes dealing with vital questions:

Who will do **what,**
when, and **where?**

Tools such as the Seven Steps of Planning can be useful at this stage. Effective delegation of the different parts of the work to be done is also very important.

The project now moves into the phase of **implementation**. As the group has moved from step to step, they will have moved through a process of **Vision, Belief and Planning**. It is important to realise that if any step is not well done the dream will never become a reality, the project will peter out. It is very enlightening at times to reflect on projects which have not succeeded and identify at which point the fatal weakness occurred.

i. **The Decline**

When we first start to implement a new project, if the different steps in the process of development have been well done, there will be united effort, confidence and enthusiasm about the project. There will be no doubt that it is worthwhile. But gradually doubts will begin to creep in. It is essential to stop from time to time to reflect, as a group, on what we are doing, evaluating our work, **checking on goals, roles and relationships** and dealing honestly with any doubts that may have arisen.

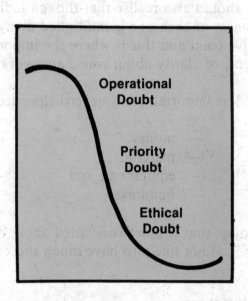

Operational Doubt

Priority Doubt

Ethical Doubt

j. **Operational Doubt**

The first level of doubt likely to arise is on the operational level. Is the programme working well? Is the organisation efficient? If there are problems these can be dealt with, and the project will continue to grow in range and effectiveness, towards the guiding star.

k. **Priority Doubts**

It is possible that the doubts may be at a deeper level. People may be starting to question whether the priorities are right. For instance in developing basic Christian communities some might begin to feel that the communities are coming together to pray all right, but they are not doing much to put love into practice and are ignoring some extremely pressing needs of their neighbours. On the other hand, they may be getting totally preoccupied with practical projects and be ignoring the spiritual side. In either case, it is important that all members feel free to question and if necessary re-establish the priorities.

j. **Ethical Doubts**

It is also possible that at some point, people who have started a project in all good faith, begin to question whether that project may be doing some serious harm. For instance it is possible for Christian communities to become extremely self-centred, and develop rivalry or antagonism within the wider community. Nothing human is totally free from sin and error. Projects that were necessary and appropriate at one period may cause harm at a later date. It is normal that needs and priorities change. It is a sign of great courage when groups and the leaders involved are prepared to take very seriously the levels of doubt that are arising about a project. If harm is being done in some way it may be possible to reshape the project and chart a true course again. At times it may definitely be best for the project to come to an end. To decide to close a project does not mean that it has failed or that it has not done very valuable work in its own time.

If such a project has arisen within a group with an on-going life, such as the Church, this is a moment when it is really important to cut back on activity, to take time for prayer, reflection, and renewal.

It is a **time to dream a new dream**.

> to dream the impossible dream
> to fight the unbeatable foe
> to bear with unbearable sorrow
> to run where the brave dare not go
> to right the unrightable wrong
> to love, pure and chaste, from afar
> to try when your arms are too weary
> to reach the unreachable star.
> This is my quest
> to follow that star,
> no matter how hopeless,
> no matter how far
> to fight for the right,
> without question or pause,
> to be willing to march into hell
> for a heavenly cause.
> And I know, if I'll only be true
> to this glorious quest,
> that my heart will lie peaceful and still,
> when I'm called to my rest.
> And the world will be better for this
> that one man, scorned and covered with scars,
> still strove, with his last ounce of courage,
> to reach the unreachable stars.
>
> — Don Quixote in
> **The Man of La Mancha**

2.   EXERCISES ON CLARIFYING VISION

a.   Visual presentation and/or Common Statement

One way to help a group clarify their vision is to ask them to express it in a diagram or picture. This should be done in groups of 4 or 5 people, so that everyone can be actively involved. If the group is larger, some are sure to be passive.

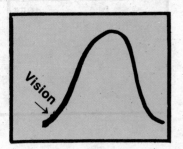

Procedure

i.   Ask them first to discuss, 'What is your vision of the Church in Development?' or 'What is your vision of our movement?'

ii.   Make a symbol, diagram or picture which represents this vision. Each group then puts up their poster and a spokesperson for the group explains it.

iii.   Each group is then asked to prepare a statement expressing the common vision in the light of all the posters. These statements are written on newsprint and put up around the room.

iv. Each person goes around reading the statements, and underlining the phrases which they feel are particularly important.

v. A small committee is then asked to take the statement with most underlining and use this as a basis for a common statement, including key points from other statements which may not have been included.

vi. This statement is then read to the whole group for affirmation.

b. **The historical story**

Many organisations, religious communities and groups have a long and eventful history together, in the course of which their original vision and values have emerged in many different ways. Some people know some parts of the history and others, other parts. A common review of the history helps to remind everybody of the vision and values, and to develop a sense of solidarity. It also highlights changes in values.

Procedures

Step 1 Small groups of 5 – 7, meet together to look at the history of the group as they have experienced it, in the following way.

'Starting from **today and working back in time,** list those events in your history which seem most significant to you.'

The decisive events can be negative or positive. Each small group is given three or four sheets of newsprint on which to draw a time line through the centre of the connected pages. Example:

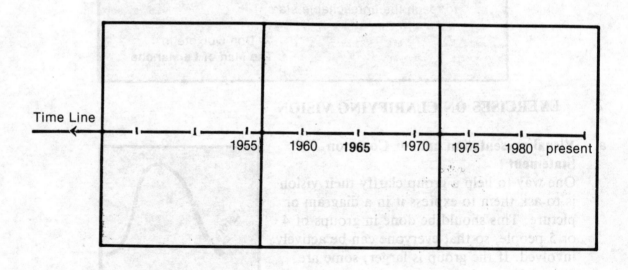

There may be disagreement as to dates or perceptions of these events. However, each group should seek a minimum of consensus as to the historically significant events as they remember them. (Do not permit references to minutes of meetings, pamphlets, etc.)

Time: This step takes about 2 hours.

Step 2   Again starting with the present and moving back in time together, the small groups share their perceptions of the historically significant events in the large group. These are recorded on large pieces of newsprint. This step needs a facilitator who can stop the process at moments to ask people to elaborate on key statements they make; asking for stories beyond some events; clarifying points but not interrupting.

You will need one or two people to write on the newsprint. These people should use very clear and simple print and be people who can quickly pick up the key words which the members are using without going into debates on dates, or spellings, etc.

Time: 45 mins. to 1½ hours, depending on the group.

Step 3   Meaning

Either in the same groups or mixed groups of 5 or 6 people, they are asked to discuss:

> **'What insights does our history give us?'**
> (or What is the meaning of these events for us?)

Together each small group prepares one statement which they put on newsprint.

Time: About 45 minutes.

Step 4   All of the meaning statements are put up on the front wall and read out to the whole group. Then the same small groups each choose one of the 'meaning statements', not necessarily their own, to work on further. The members of the group then:

> **Brainstorm for 10 minutes on the worst possibilities, any time, any place, if these aspects of our reality continue into the future.**
> (Note: No discussion of the brainstorming is allowed.)

Step 5   Having completed that task, each small group is given the next task:

> **Brainstorm for 10 minutes on the best possibilities, any time, any place, if these aspects of our reality continue into our future.**
> (Note: Again no discussion on these points.)

Step 6 After these two brainstorming sessions, each person is asked to individually list five of the

a. **best** possibilities, and/or

b. **reversed worst** possibilities (that is, the positive value recognised in the negative fear. For example, 'We may all split up and go our own ways.' Reversed equals: 'We must find practical ways of forstering unity in the group.'

These appear as **guidelines or principles** for the movement or organisation. Each person shares his/her list with the others in the small group. Each small group now develops from the individual lists, a group list of 5 – 7 guidelines or principles.

The Best Possibilities
1.
2.
3.
4.
5.

Time: About 1 hour for steps 4 through 6.

Step 7 In the whole group, each small group shares their list of guidelines or principles for the movement or organisation.

Step 8 **The emergence of directional goals**

If the group you are working with is a policy-making body, and has the authority to make decisions for the whole movement or organisation, a process of ranking each of the above guidelines and principles needs to come next. This can be done simply by giving a number e.g. of 10 to the item of highest importance, of 9 to that of next importance down to '0' which would mean, 'not acceptable'.

All the participants have now had an opportunity to rank their guidelines and principles. The total group can then reflect together on their work and their top priorities, which will need follow-up. The directional goals have been emerging out of this process.

Depending on the nature of the organisation, smaller task groups, or planning groups, may be designated to formulate particular policies or objectives, and then bring them back to the group. This is necessary to ensure they are carrying out the group's wishes.

The historisizing process takes at least one day and up to three days to complete. It is best used when a group has had little time in past years to reflect communally on their own values and vision. It is also useful when there have been some conflicts and polarisation within the organisation, or when policies seem outdated or unreal to some members.

3. VALUES AND ASSUMPTIONS

In the vision statements, many words will be used that have different meanings for different people. Information, opinions, and feelings all play a part in forming attitudes and thus each individual has an understanding of what is being said, based on certain assumptions.

In development work, a number of assumptions need discussion, in order to clarify the values of the group. In a workshop, it is important to move from 'vision', to clarifying the assumptions behind some of the key words people have used in their vision statements, for example, equality, shared responsibility, unity, self-reliance, etc.

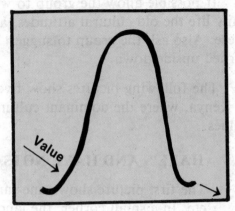

The following are only a few of the assumptions which repeatedly came up in development work in Kenya. These and others can be explored in a workshop.

UPSIDE DOWN CODES

Every culture, in every time, is challenged by the Gospel. By this we mean the Good News of Jesus, as God reveals it, both in the Bible and in the life of the Christian community. All of us neea to look carefully at the values and customs of our particular culture in the light of the Gospel.

In all cultures we will find that there are some values that are deeply affirmed by the Gospel (e.g. the spirit of hospitality in African culture; the awareness of our call to co-create the world in western culture). However in other respects the Gospel turns the values of the world upside down. This is particularly clear in the Beatitudes, which provide us with a totally new standard of happiness and success.

As the Christian community, and as individuals, we are called to a Prophetic role in the world, to **denounce** what is evil and **announce** the new — the possible — the good.

In each culture we need to identify those values, which the life and teaching of Jesus call most deeply into question. These will be different in different countries. For example, in India where we first developed this code, the first value the Indian Christians said must be challenged was a 'Caste', that is, valueing a person according to the caste into which they were born, and not recognising the equal dignity of all, stemming from the fact that we are all children of God.

Procedure

Once the values that need challenging have been identified, a picture is made of a very typical scene reflecting that value.

Discussion Questions after each picture:

i. What do you see in this picture?
ii. What attitudes and values do the people involved show?
iii. Are these values consistent with the Gospel? (Or in our code of conduct, or other documents of the country.)
   Give examples from the Bible which show how these values are challenged or turned upside down, by Jesus, other passages or documents.

Turn the picture upside down, and put beside it another picture showing an alternative attitude and value.

If possible allow the group to work out other concrete ways which express in daily life the old cultural attitudes, and how the values of the Gospel might change these. Also ask the group to suggest other values current in society, which should be turned upside down.

The following pictures show five of the values which were chosen for discussion in Kenya, where the dominant culture contains a mixture of traditional and western values.

1.   HAVE'S AND HAVE NOTS versus EQUAL SHARING

a.   The first picture shows one family with a very large house, farm, car, etc. In a small corner, the landless labourers are crowded very close together in miserable little huts.

b.   A contrasting scene in which each family has roughly equal sized farm and a reasonably good house.

Readings
Julius Nyerere, **Freedom and Development**, 'The Plea of the Poor', pp. 214 – 228.
Arusha Declaration, **Ujamaa**, p. 36.
Samora Machel Speaks, pp. 6 – 8.

Scripture References

The story of the Rich Man, Dives and the Beggar, Lazarus (Luke 16:19 – 26).
The Early Christians sharing all their possessions (Acts 4:32 – 37)
Sermon on the Mount (Matthew 5:40 – 42, 6:19 – 21, Luke 6:30 – 36).
The Magnificat (Luke 1:51 – 53). Response to the needs of others (James 2:14 – 16).

2. **SUPERIORITY OF THE EDUCATED** versus **RESPECT FOR THE WISDOM OF ALL**

a. The first picture shows a proud, well-dressed educated man, 'talking down' to a poor woman who despises herself.

b. The second picture shows a man and a woman looking at one another with mutual respect, no matter how educated or dressed.

Readings
Canaan Banana, **The Gospel According to the Ghetto**, pp. 69 – 72.
Ngungi wa Thiong'o, **Education for a National Culture**, Zimbabwe Publishing House, pp. 12 – 13.
Amilcar Cabral, **Unity and Struggle**, pp. 73, 246.
Julius Nyerere, **Ujamaa**, pp. 13 & 103.

Scripture References
Jesus rejoices in the wisdom of the 'Unlearned', Luke 10:21, 23 – 24.
St. Paul recognises the limitation of the 'wisdom of the wise'. I Cor. 1:18 – 29.
Honouring the Dignity of all, James 2:1 – 7.
Jesus discusses theology with a Samaritan woman at a well and allows her to bring his message to others, John 4:1 – 41.

3.   **CONCENTRATED POWER** versus **SHARED RESPONSIBILITY**

a. The first shows a very 'big' politician addressing a crowd of people. They look passive and bored.

b. A small group in a meeting and everyone is actively involved in sharing ideas and making decisions.

Readings
Julius Nyerere, **Freedom and Development**, p. 179.
Arusha Declaration, **Ujamaa**, p. 13 f.
Samora Machel Speaks, p. 19.
Amilcar Cabral, **Unity and Struggle**, p. 247 – 248.

Scripture References
Jesus shares responsibility for the Kingdom with simple country people (Matthew 10:1 – 14).
Jesus shares responsibility with the 72 disciples, (Luke 10:1 – 12, 17 – 24)
Authority at Service (Matt. 20:25 – 28)
Moses shares responsibility, (Deuteronomy 1:9 – 18).

4. **TRIBALISM** versus **UNITY**

    a.   The first picture shows each different racial group or tribe separated in a different circle living in 'their own little world'. This can be done using stick figures of different colours in each circle.

    b.   A small group is enjoying a meal together around one large round table and the picture shows people of all different colours and tribes.

Readings
Julius Nyerere, **Freedom and Development**, pp. 370 – 371.
Canaan Banana, **The Gospel According to the Ghetto**, p. 68.
Amilcar Cabral's Speeches, **Unity and Struggle**, pp. 28 – 31.

Scripture References
'That they all may be One', (John 17:20 – 23)
The Kingdom compared to a Great Feast (Luke 14:12 – 17, 21 – 23)
You are All One Body in Christ (I Cor. 12 – 31)

5. FATALISM versus RESPONSIBILITY

a. The first picture can show irresponsible driving. Either a drunken driver has gone off the road, knocking over a passer-by. Or, a car passing on a 'blind' curve, has caused an accident. It has collided with an on-coming car and there are many dead bodies lying on the ground. What do people say? 'Shauri ya Mungu'. 'It's God's Will'.

b. In the second picture the same scene is repeated, but the driver is going more slowly, or waiting responsibly till he can see the whole road before passing.

Readings
Paulo Freire, **Education for Critical Consciousness,** pp. 12 — 20.
Canaan Banana, **The Gospel According to the Ghetto,** p. 71.

Scripture References
Whatever you would like others to do to you. (Matthew 7:12).
'Am I my brother's keeper?' (Genesis 4:8 — 12)

> ### Courage
>
> "We must have the courage to look each other straight in the eye, because our party can only be led by men and women who do not have to lower their eyes before anyone. . . .
> "The tendency of some comrades is to monopolise leadership for themselves. They decide everything, they do not consult the views of anyone at their side. This cannot go on, for two heads are always worth more than one, even if one is clever and the other is stupid."
>
> Amilcar Cabral
> **Unity and Struggle**, p. 73.

a. **Basic Christian Communities**

(It would be equally important to explore deeply the assumptions about values in a co-operative or a social movement.)

The AMECEA Bishop's conference in 1973, and then again in 1976 and 1979, have stressed that fostering Basic Christian Communities is one of the key goals for the Church in AMECEA countries. Because the concept is new (though it is really the oldest idea of Christian communities), people with different backgrounds, education and culture, interpret differently what 'Basic Christian Communities' means to them concretely.

Code

One way to help a group discuss this idea is to see and then discuss the two films, *New Day in Brazil* and *These Men Are Dangerous*. We have found it best to show the films one evening, and discuss them the following morning.

Possible Discussion Questions

1. What struck you most about the films?
2. What were the most important elements of the Basic Christian Community in Sao Paulo?
3. Are some of these key elements already happening in our own communities? Can some of them begin to happen? How?
4. What major insights did you gain from the second film?

"I believe that as Christians we ought to preoccupy ourselves with a search for a viable community and this we can do by joining hands with all progressive forces of change in the world. Ours is the task of finding new areas of common interest with those struggling to bring about new social orders. If we do not participate in the process we have no way of influencing the outcome. The simple fact of life is that we either influence change, or are influenced by it. I often wonder what we mean when we talk glibly of the kingdom of God on earth. How many Christians ever bother to translate into specific terms what this kingdom ought to be? Have Christians ever exploited the rich heritage in the Bible that can offer a sound basis for evolving a humanistic ideology? How many of us have ever taken seriously the example of the early Christians who practised socialism? According to Acts 2:44 — 45, it is quite evident that a society built on the shifting sands of individualism must give way to a society of collective living."

Canaan Banana
The Gospel According to the Ghetto, p. 50

b. Self-Reliance

A borrowed fiddle does not finish a tune.
— Zimbabwean proverb

In most situations of dependence, 'self-reliance' is a very generative theme. Government, Church and community groups all show interest in discussing, 'can we become self-reliant?' Many projects and programs are mainly sponsored and financed from outside resources.

The following code was developed to help laity, priests, and bishops to face the situation of dependence as honestly as possible.

Code: The Co-ordinator's Nightmare

This is a short play that shows many different types of local requests coming to a development co-ordinator. The co-ordinator is asleep on a table and having a nightmare. Slowly, a person comes and asks for salaries for social workers. The co-ordinator responds, "I'll ask Cebemo." Then another person comes and requests a car. The co-ordinator responds by saying (in his sleep), "I'll ask Misereor." More and more people come, faster and faster, asking for more and more things. The co-ordinator continues to respond thinking of all the different outside funding agencies which could give money.

Suddenly there is a knock on the door, a man appears with a telegram. The co-ordinator wakes up, reads the telegram which says,

"We regret to inform you, but Kenya (Zimbabwe, Nigeria) is no longer a priority for aid from overseas agencies. Other countries are in far greater need. We wish you luck in becoming self-reliant."

The play ends with the co-ordinator just staring at the telegram.

After the play, Matthew 7:24 – 27, about the house which was built upon sand instead of on a good foundation is read.

Discussion questions

In small groups, these questions are discussed:
1. What did you see happening in the play?
2. In what way was the 'development house' built on sand?
3. What can we do to make sure we build on solid rock?

These responses can be shared in the whole group. Then in regional, parish, or very local groups, the last two questions are discussed.
4. How can we really aim at self-reliance in terms of:
   — personnel (voluntary or part-time)
   — money
   — equipment.
5. If limited funds are available, should they be used for:
   a. a few full-time workers,
   b. twice as many part-time workers,
   c. training of voluntary workers and groups?

These last two questions need to be discussed in depth, and can lead to some clear guidelines and recommendations for a program and/or a diocese.

c. **Leadership and the Use of Power**

To exercise leadership is to exercise power. Many Christians have mixed feelings about power because it has so often been abused. It is important that the group reflect on some of their assumptions about power.

Procedure

They can be asked to brainstorm, first in small groups, then describe in the whole group (using pictures and flannelgraph) the different types of power that they recognize. It often happens that far more negative aspects than positive aspects are mentioned.

Input on Different Types of Power

The following input can be given as a summary or as the basis for further discussion.

1. **The Power of God and the Power of Human Beings**

In all of nature and throughout the Bible, we see the creative and the re-creative power of God. Genesis describes beautifully how He made the world and He made human beings as the crown of His creation. In making us in His image, He shared with us the imagination, the creative energy and the ability to shape our lives, our environment and our community.

"God created human beings in the image of himself
in the image of God He created them
male and female He created them.
God blessed them, saying to them,
'Be fruitful, multiply,
fill the earth and conquer it.
Be rulers of the fish and the sea,
the birds of the heaven,
and all the living animals on the earth. . . .'"

Later we read, God took the man and settled him in the garden to cultivate it and take care of it. The naming of the animals is another symbol of the power God gives to us.

Put a picture of a man and a woman in the centre of the flannelgraph. This vision of human beings, called to share in the creative work of God, 'building the earth', co-creators of the world, and of one another, is beautifully developed in the writings of Teilhard de Chardin.

2.   The Power of the Group

As individuals we each have a certain amount of power, to shape things and make things happen. But human beings were not made to live alone. In the image of the Trinity, we were made to live in community, and far greater power resides, by right, and by fact, in the group than in any isolated individual. Much later the power of the Holy Spirit was promised by Jesus and resides in the Christian community as a whole, though it also operates actively beyond this community. (See Documents of Vatican II, especially Lumen Gentium and Gaudium et Spes.)

Beside the man and woman put pictures of two or three other people. The power of the group depends upon unity. As soon as sin breaks the unity of the group, its power is very much reduced, and then individuals begin to acquire different types of power.

3.   The Power of Force

In some situations, physical strength becomes the chief source of power. Men use not only their own strength, but weapons, armaments, armies, police and prisons to impose their will upon others.

At one point in history the invention of gunpowder gave the Western world immense power over many other countries. Today, in many parts of the world, the majority of the people are powerless in situations that are dominated by force.

Put up a picture of an army man with a gun.

4.   The Power of Wealth

In other situations a relatively small number of people have gained control of the sources of wealth, and they use their economic power to maintain a situation which is to their advantage. Money gives them the Power of Reward and Punishment. Those who own the land and the factories have the power to 'hire and fire' their workers, so others become dependent and powerless. The proverb, 'He who pays the piper, calls the tune,' is usually true.

In very many places the rich make laws which are entirely to the advantage of the rich. When there is a shortage of jobs, or other things people need and want, the way lies wide open for corruption and the rich can rapidly become richer and more powerful. Where the wealth of a country is evenly distributed among all the people, there is also a much more even sharing of power.

Put up a picture of a fat rich man holding money in his hands.

5.   The Power of Appointment

The government of a country has power, acquired in different ways. Sometimes through force, sometimes through those with economic power, occasionally conferred by the people in a truly democratic process. In the local situation those appointed by the government; the magistrates, the district commissioners, the educational officers, etc., have power, sometimes used for the good of the community, sometimes used for their own benefit.

If there is a good structure and people are fully aware of their own rights, then these appointed officials are accountable to the people, and have far less opportunity to abuse their power.

Put up a picture of a government officer next to Parliament buildings.

6. **The Church also has power,** not only that coming direct from the Holy Spirit, but also that which comes from being a highly organised, world-wide institution, with many highly qualified personnel, and much wealth at her disposal.

She also has the power of appointment through a hierarchical structure, which reaches down through the bishops and parish priests to the catechists at the village level, and various positions of lay responsibility at diocesan and national levels. It is important to analyse how the Church uses these different types of power in different situations.

Put up a picture of St. Peter's Church in Rome and a Bishop with Mitre and Crozier.

7. **The Power of Knowledge**

Those with special knowledge and expertise, e.g. doctors, lawyers, theologians, teachers have also a special power. It can be used for the good of the whole community. However, this power has been growing constantly because of the immense faith, sometimes a blind faith, which people now have in the 'expert', and in the educational system which produces the expert. The present educational system has caused many people to distrust the knowledge they have from their own experience, and depend completely on advice of the 'experts', though this has frequently proved wrong. Knowledge, like wealth, needs to be widely and evenly distributed, if people are to keep the independence required for human dignity, and the 'haves' prevented from taking advantage of the 'have nots'.

Put up a picture of a university graduate in a cap holding a certificate.

8. **The Power of Expertise**

Other forms of expertise also give people a form of power. The car mechanic, the builder, the electrician, the nurse, the farmer, the engineer, all have the power to shape the life of the community.

Put up a picture of a mechanic fixing a car or a builder at work.

9.   The Power of Love and Service

There are some people who, with no formal position, and not mainly on account of their special knowledge or expertise, have acquired an immense influence and power simply through their loving service and complete commitment to the needs of people. Amilcar Cabral, Sister Teresa of Calcutta, Gandhi, Dom Helder Camara are outstanding examples of such influence and power and there are many others in the history of the world and the Church.

Put up a picture of Sr. Teresa or Gandhi.

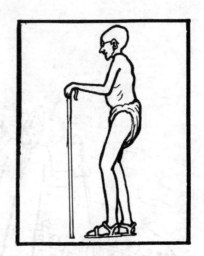

10   The Recovery of the Power of the Group

One of the main forms of loving service needed in the world today is to help ordinary people recover what they have lost or what has been taken from them. Only then will they be able to regain their rights and ability to shape their lives, their communities, their environment as they want them to be. In many situations the people are powerless unless they are united and organised. The role of the animator is to help them recover their power by building unity and trust, finding common goals, and organising effectively to achieve these goals.

Put up a picture of an animator, a simple unobtrusive person in the middle of the group.

Procedure continued

After this input, it is important to give the group an opportunity to buzz and then to ask questions or make comments. If possible, give them an opportunity to identify the different types of power that are operating in a situation they know well, e.g. a district or parish, the Church, the nation.

It is also useful to analyse sometimes the different types of power that different groups have at their disposal, e.g. Priests/Laity, men/women.

> **In what ways do we need to empower people if we are to move towards 'Shared Responsibility'?**

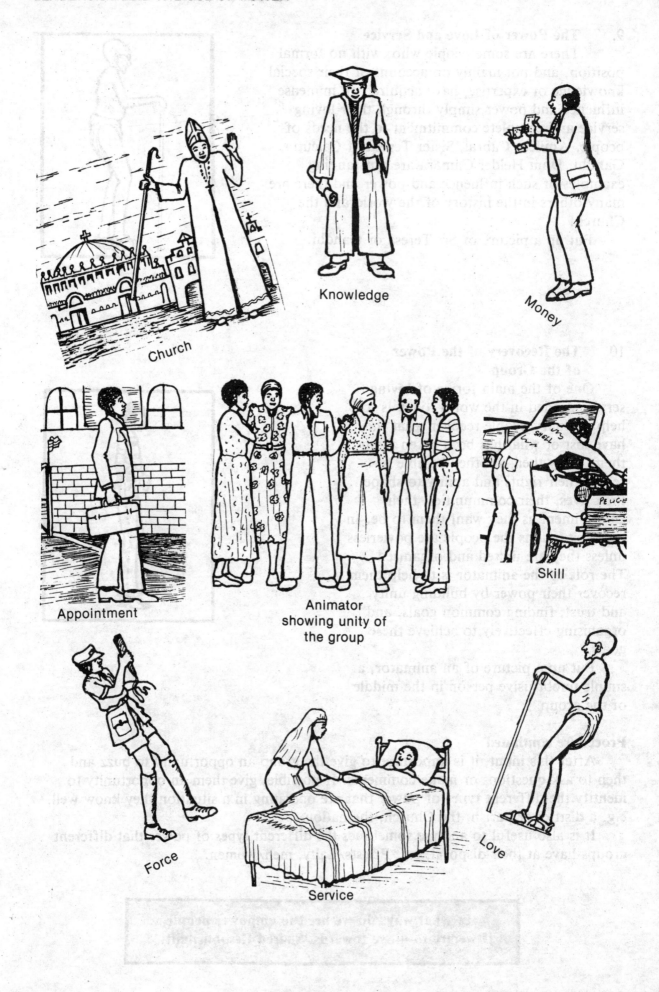

Church

Knowledge

Money

Appointment

Animator
showing unity of
the group

Skill

Force

Service

Love

d.   **Power Struggles and Power Vacuums: The Anthills**

The following exercise is to help people to reflect on their own motivations. It can be used to challenge people where there is a tendency to scramble for powerful positions.

Input and Drawings

Draw a picture (along the bottom of the blackboard or along the bottom of several sheets of newsprint put side by side), of everyday life in a village. It should include many little huts, people working in their fields, carrying water, herding cattle, cooking, children playing, old people sitting in the sun, some people carrying a sick person off on a stretcher, chickens and goats.

This can be done as a group mural asking people to draw huts and activities in a village. In the background one can draw something familiar like Mt. Kenya, Mt. Kilimanjaro, or the sea. The livelier the scene the better. There should also be 3 or 4 prominent anthills.

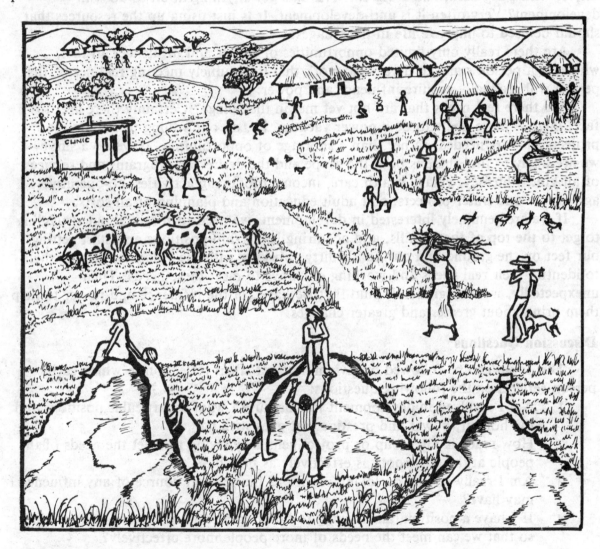

Ask the group, what they see in the picture?
    Do villages like this still exist?
Life has gone on like this in many places for a number of generations. As different needs are recognized in the community, different institutions are established. These are represented by the anthills. They represent schools, clinics, women's clubs, school boards, parish councils, development committees, youth clubs, county councils etc.

Gradually these institutions have introduced paid jobs, and positions of leadership such as headmasters, county councillors, M.P.s, chairmen of various committees, co-ordinators of this and of that.

The institutions are established in the first place to meet the needs of the people. However, soon the positions are seen as platforms of power. **A tremendous scramble begins to get to the top**. It is like the children's game, where one stands on top of an anthill or table and chants, "I'm the king of the castle, and you're the dirty rascal." Then all the others try to push him off and take his place.

The people at the top of the anthills are hanging on to their positions, as chairperson of this, or head of that, or secretary of this. Meanwhile, others are doing their utmost to push them off and take their places. Of course where these are paid jobs, the main motivation is that everybody wants to get more money. But why is there so much rivalry and struggle for the unpaid positions?

These are pure power struggles. Leadership and power have become associated with having an important position with a fine sounding title, and if possible a big office, with a big desk, and a big car. Has this got anything at all to do with development? Very often it is anti-development. It is just using up the resources that should be used to improve life in the villages.

Are there really only limited opportunities of power and influence? In fact, wherever a person starts to do a valid work that is genuinely meeting real needs, that person will gradually acquire influence and power.

Are there real needs that are not yet met in the village? Certainly there are. In fact, there is more likely to be **a power vacuum**, i.e. no one willing to initiate the projects that are needed, rather than a shortage of opportunities. If we do a survey we are likely to find there is both the scope and the desire for programs and services of all kinds; literacy, village health care, income producing activities, co-operative agriculture and water projects, and adult education and planning of all sorts.

If we are genuinely interested in development, we need to forget about struggling to get to the top of the anthills, and acquiring leadership positions and start getting our feet on the ground and our hands dirty, working with the villagers, helping them to identify their real needs and working out ways to meet these needs. Then unexpectedly, we may gradually find that we have got the influence and power to help them bring about greater and greater changes.

Discussion Questions

This input can be followed by five minutes of silent reflection in which each person reflects on the following questions:

1. Am I involved in development just because I want a particular position, and the honour, power and prestige that goes with it?
2. How much is my group or project genuinely trying to meet the needs of the people at the grassroots as effectively as possible?
3. Am I really relying on loving service as the primary source of any influence I may have?
4. If I have a position, am I trying to build up a team and share responsibility so that we can meet the needs of more people more effectively?

Readings

After the quiet reflection, one can end with the reading from Matthew 20:20 – 28 on authority as service. This could also be used as the basic theme of the worship that day. Other readings could be on Collective Leadership by Cabral found in Chapter 6 of this book.

e.   **Accountability**

Being responsible for development work means in fact being **responsible to people**. Everyone working with people needs structures to enable them to work at their best. The support and the challenge of our stewardship, and accountability for all of our time and money, is
critical for **building trust and unity in groups**.

If all the people to whom I am responsible, know my work in relation to the structures they themselves have helped to make, then the task of each person is clear and out in the open. Any group in the structure can hold any other person or group accountable for their actions.

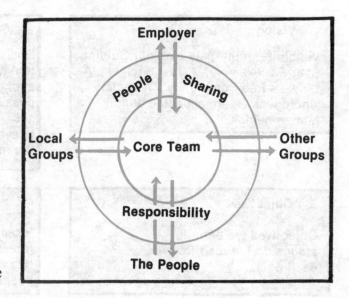

The following diagram is only an example. Each group or person can put themselves in the middle and map out who they would be accountable to. One can see that the core team is responsible to:

(a)   those nearest them,
(b)   to their employers or the hierarchy,
(c)   to the people at the grassroots,
(d)   to other development groups,
(e)   to other groups related to the area one is serving.

Discussion Questions

1. Do you agree in principle, that accountability must happen on all levels as seen in the diagram?
2. If so, how can this be put into practice in our own situation?
3. What structures are needed to ensure accountability to every other group concerned?

4. SETTING GOALS

We must be clear with groups about
the difference between:

— Vision
— Goals
— Objectives
— Programs

1. **Vision**	2. **Goals**
Vision if our ultimate aim, our Guiding Star. For example, 'A Just Society', 'A Disease-free Community', 'A society where women are accepted as full human beings'.	Goals state the particular situation we hope to have reached by a specific date. They are a long range **destination**, but one that is possible to achieve. (E.g. 'By the end of 1984, we plan to have a clean water supply in every village.') Goals show clearly why the group exists.
3. **Objectives**	4. **Programs**
Objectives are definite stages on the road towards each goal.	Programs are detailed plans of **how** we intend to reach the goal, e.g. 'We will begin by recruiting a team to do a survey of the needs'.

The movement of a group from vision,
through clarifying major assumptions,
to setting goals
is not any easy process, but is essential if anything
significant is to be achieved.

Procedure

a. Ask each team to read through their visions statements and go through each assumption they have discussed around the key words in their vision statement. At this point, there can be a quiet period for the individuals to reflect on:

Do we understand our vision?
Do we agree with the assumptions behind this vision?
This discussion is useful to draw together all the work done so far in the group.

b. Now ask the group to look at the vision statement and see whether in that statement there are some ideas **which are expressed as needs,** e.g. 'There is a need for. . . .' These need statements must be taken into account when making goals.

c. The group is now asked to make a goal statement(s). **Goals are points of arrival, not actions to be taken.** Goals are achievements which we will be able to see or measure by a particular time.

The animators must check with the groups that they are not writing vision statements, but concrete and achievable goals.

5.   **PLANNING**

A number of different planning tools are
found in Chapter 7 in this book. The following
planning guidelines are more complex, but can also
be very helpful to large organisations.

a.   **Planning Checklist***

This tool can be used by a group to see if their
projects or programs have done proper planning in
relation to building a supportive and responsive
structure.

1.   In beginning new programs of projects check:
  — how the decision has been made to begin the project — consensus
    of the community or a one-man/woman show?
  — are goals clear and acceptable to all or are there conflicting goals?
  — have assumptions been clarified to meet people's satisfaction?
  — is there a framework for quick communication?
  — is there a definite direction?
  — is there clarity about the size, nature and complexity of the project?

2.   In checking existing programs:
  — is there a method of checking the original goals in relation to
    practice?
  — is there a method of checking the program in relation to the
    original goals?
  — if they are not consistent, have the goals changed?
  — are these changed goals acceptable to everyone, or do we need to
    change the program to put it back on the road towards the original
    goals?
  — has a method been established to test the effectiveness of the
    program?
  — are there procedures to change the program and get participants'
    reactions?
  — is there a way to test the level of support for the program?
  — how has work been divided? Who decided these procedures and is
    there agreement about work divisions?

3.   Checking the Leadership
  — who is thinking through problems on the project and new
    directions?
  — who is developing commitment to the project among the people,
    with other groups, in the structures involved, etc.?
  — who is responsible for preparing meetings, putting ideas in order,
    and designing meetings so they can be run most effectively with
    maximum participation?

* From *Leadership: The Responsible Exercise of Power*, MDI Group, Cincinnati, Ohio, USA.

b.   **Agenda Building**

In many organisations, the chairperson assumes (s)he is responsible to make the agenda. One has seen many group leaders lose commitment of the people because the people have not participated in developing their own agenda.

1.   How to Make a Common Agenda

Of course, a chairperson or a secretary may have a number of items for an agenda because they have been in communication with a number of people. This is valid. But to build group unity and responsibility, it is useful to ask the group members, in 2's or 3's, to make a list of the major items they think must be on the agenda for this particular meeting.

The facilitator then writes on newsprint all agenda items which come from the group, adding his or her own agenda points which may not have been mentioned by the group.

It is amazing how the group will usually mention all the items that the chairperson thought of him/herself. This way of making a common agenda is another **practical way of showing trust in the group.**

2.   Clarifying Agenda Points

We have all been in meetings where we seem to be going around and around in circles and only later do we see that it would have been very easy to deal with the topic in 5 minutes. This is often caused by a lack of clarity about what we want to do with a topic — either as the presenter of the topic, or as a group.

Two things can help a group to move through agenda items more effectively.

   a.   The person who want to put something on the agenda (the presenter) must state to the chairperson and the group what (s)he is going to do:
   — I am giving you information.
   — I am making an evaluation.
   — I am making a recommendation.
   — I am reporting a decision by X group.
   — I am reporting an action by X group.
   b.   The presenter must also be clear what (s)he then expects of the group.
   'I request of this group:
   — to receive information
   — to receive information and evaluate that information
   — to make a decision
   — to delegate people for implementing a particular action.
   The presenter must be clear that such action is within the authority of that group.

c.   **Taking Responsibility**

In most planning models, the important task of deciding who is to take responsibility for different tasks is key to whether plans will be implemented.

The more people are involved from the beginning (in setting the vision, the goals and deciding the kinds of programs they need) the more involvement there will be from members throughout the implementation of the program.

d.   **Decision-Making**

Decision-making is a crucial moment in an organisation and once the preparatory work has been done thoroughly, the actual decision needs to be taken quickly.

As we have seen in Chapter 7, and the Seven Steps of Planning model, a number of steps are necessary before a decision is made:

— the group is asked to brainstorm alternative proposals,
— each proposal is then discussed stating the advantages and disadvantages of each proposal,
— each of the proposals are written on newsprint and should be numbered (or lettered).

1.   Negative Voting

One method of helping a group come to a decision is called the negative voting method. The list of alternatives are in front of the group. The group now **proceeds to eliminate alternatives by negative voting,** that is by voting against those alternatives which they wish to eliminate. If there are less than seven alternatives, the process will be fast. With seven alternatives, there would be three rounds of negative voting:

— **round one** each person has three negative votes and thus can vote against the three alternatives they like least. The three getting the most negative votes are eliminated.
— **round two** each person has two negative votes to eliminate the two alternatives still liked least. The two getting the most negative votes are eliminated.
— **round three** leaves only two alternatives and at this point, the group will **shift to positive voting**.

When only two alternatives are left, the group changes their voting process to vote for the one of the two alternatives they like most. After the vote the chairperson states the decision that has been made.

If the vote is a close one, it is best to state that no decision has been made since such a close vote indicates a split and therefore the group will be unlikely to get full commitment to the outcome.

Sometimes the last two alternatives differ only on operational details, but are basically the same decision. The chairperson may note this and test whether or not the group wishes to accept the basic decision and delegate the details to a sub-committee or the chairperson.

If the vote is not close, but also not unanimous (e.g. 10 to 2), then a decision has been made, but the chairperson should check with those who voted against the decision to see if they are willing to abide by the decision.

DECISION MAKING

2. Transferable Voting

This method of voting can be used in choosing alternative proposals, or when voting for people to take special responsibilities. It has the advantage of balancing the votes, and stops a clique from 'stacking' the votes.

Preference

1. *Joan*
2. *Ruth*
3. *Tom*
4. *Brian*
5. *Dick*
6. *Sophie*
7. *David*
8. *Jane*
9. *John*

If you were voting for a chairperson, each person is asked to vote for **as many people as possible** in the order of preference.

For example, I might vote for the nine people in a rank order of my preference as shown on the diagram.

The counting of the votes is done by eliminating those who receive the least votes on the first count, and transferring these votes to the second choice of the person voting. Again, eliminate those who receive the least votes on the second count, and transfer the votes, etc.

Names	1 count	2 count	3 count	4 count	5 count
John	8 votes	+1 = 9	0 = 9	+2 = 11	+2 = 13
Jane	6 votes	0 = 6	0 = 6	0 = 6	out
Joan	6 votes	+2 = 8	+2 =10	+4 = 14	+4 = 18
Brian	3 votes	0 = 3	0 = 3	out	out
Dick	3 votes	0 = 3	0 = 3	out	out
David	2 votes	0 = 2	out	out	out
Sophie	1 vote	out	out	out	out
Tom	1 vote	out	out	out	out
Ruth	1 vote	out	out	out	out
	31	31	31	31	31

The winner is Joan on round 5.

The person who wins should accumulate over half the votes of the total number of persons voting. Ruth, Tom and Sophie were eliminated on the first count. Take those ballots and transfer each vote to the name of the next person who is on list above. For example, if you voted for Ruth as first choice and John as second choice, since now Ruth is out (because she has too few votes) then your second choice is put onto the votes in the second round (your second choice is John and he gets your vote on the second count).

B.   Roles

1.   Leadership Styles

One of the key elements enabling people to come to realise their own potential and to have self-respect, is their relationship to the leader of their group.

If a group demands that a leader do the work for them, the group is not taking responsibility for its own destiny, nor is the group able to stand on its own. This is often a fault of our own concept of leadership.

In the following chart, there are three types of leadership described:

Authoritarian Leadership
Consultative Leadership
Enabling Leadership

You will notice in the chart that different situations call for different types of leadership. For example, if the house is on fire, it is a question of survival and thus an authoritarian leadership style is appropriate.

In a new group with a strong experienced leader, while a group feels very insecure about its own identity or role in society, a consultative leadership style may be appropriate. For example a youth group may have so many personal questions about themselves and their relation to society, that the style of leadership which can help them best (at certain moments) might be one where the youth know that they can trust the leader to make decisions for them and thus they feel secure.

If the aim of a program is to help people develop maturity and responsibility, participating in making their own decisions, then the enabling style of leadership is essential.

LEADERSHIP STYLES

ENABLING LEADERSHIP participation	Leader Calls on Members to Identify Limits, Explore Situation, Make Decision	Leader maintains a facilitating role allowing members to identify situation or problem, identify limits, explore, and make decision.
	Leader Defines Limits, Calls on Members to Make Decision	Leader shares any "givens" (e.g., funds available, time parameters, etc.) and facilitates a decision by members on basis of limitations.
CONSULTATIVE LEADERSHIP security	Leader Calls on Members to Make Decision, but Holds Veto	Leader calls on group to identify situation and limitations, explore and make decision contingent on leader's veto power.
	Leader Presents Situation, Gets Input, Makes Decision	Leader identifies situation or problem and moves into a facilitating role to surface assumptions and suggestions, then moves out of facilitating role and makes a decision.
	Leader Presents Tentative Decision Subject to Change	Leader announces his "tentative" decision and announces that he is open to questions of clarification and discussion. (Dialogue with willingness to change decision if necessary.)
AUTHORITARIAN LEADERSHIP survival	Leader Presents Decision but "Sells" It to Members	Leader announces his decision, but responds on an impromptu basis with a rationale based on the questions of clarification from the members. (Dialogue with no expressed willingness to change decision.)
	Leader Presents Decision & Invites Questions of Clarification	Leader announces his decision and shares the reasons behind it, which were prepared in advance. (Monologue)
	Leader Makes Decision and Announces It	Leader announces his decision with no feeling of responsibility or accountability to share the reasons.

MD1 — Group, Ibid p. G-2

Discussion

In a workshop, an animator can give a short input on these three different styles of leadership. Each participant is given a handout on 'Leadership Styles' and in small groups, they can discuss:

1. When have you seen all 8 different forms of leadership styles used in your own situation?
2. Was each leadership style appropriate in the situation? Why or why not?
3. Should another style have been used? Why or why not?

Materials

Copies for each participant of the chart on 'Leadership Styles'.

2. **The Commitment Cycle**

    In carrying out its work, a healthy organisation progresses through a cycle:

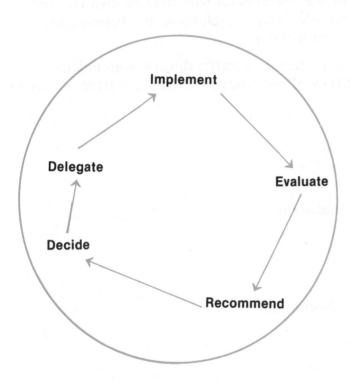

1. Evaluation
    — of the present situation in relation to the future which the group desires,
2. Recommendations
    — for the future development based on the evaluation,
3. Decisions
    — on the best course for future development, based on the recommendations,
4. Delegation
    — clearly giving responsibilities for the various tasks to be done, based on the decision.
5. Implementation
    — actions taken, based on the decisions.
6. Evaluation — of the action taken.
7. Recommendations — based on the evaluation and so forth. . . .

The roles, for individuals and different groups, change at each point in the cycle, yet each is inter-related with the other.

For example, all literacy class participants may **evaluate** the literacy program. A group of four outsiders with eight literacy animators may help evaluate the program also. The participants' evaluations may be given to a small group to summarise the findings and to make **recommendations**. The recommendations are given to the appropriate decision-making body (e.g. the district development committee). The development committee **decides** on the recommendations, **delegates** the decisions for **implementation** to the literacy co-ordinator, or the teachers, or the government, i.e. to the appropriate body.

The role of a co-ordinator is to help the group move through this cycle, timing the move to the next step at the appropriate moment, and ensuring that those who should be involved in each process can participate.

Co-ordination demands responsible adult behaviour from groups, group leaders and the co-ordinator. The aim of the co-ordinator is to move people **away from dependency,** and to help the group become self-directing, self-starting, self-controlling and self-governing.

Co-ordination fits into democratic organisations rather than authoritarian ones.

Some assumptions behind the role of co-ordinator:

a.   The co-ordinator may not be the person actually leading the group.

b.   The co-ordinator, in order to respect delegation, should not take over the tasks being performed by the delegated groups.

c.   The responsibility of the co-ordinator will often be involved, not **within** one particular role, such as evaluation, but **between** any two roles. (See diagram below.)

d.   The co-ordinator can be seen as a traffic director who judges where and how the flow of the process should move from one step to another.

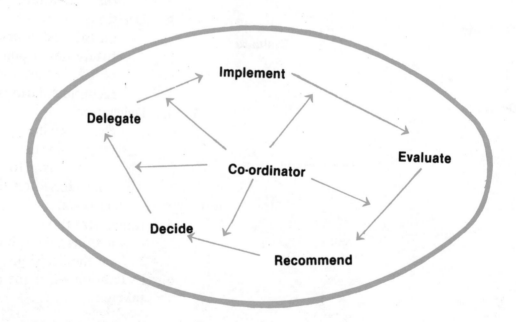

Let us look at the different parts of this cycle.

a.   **Evaluation**

As was noted earlier, evaluation takes real courage on everyone's part. Participants need courage to speak up when they have had little practice in this form of democracy. Leaders or animators need a maturity to see that feedback and greater self-knowledge about their strengths and weaknesses can help them to grow. A program may have begun with many ideals, but mistakes happen.

> "Evaluation of oneself in relation to one's goals is part of **purposeful living**. It does not imply a comparison to an absolute, or blame for not achieving what one had hoped to achieve, rather it allows one to be honest about self, group, task, and enables the organisation or movement to maintain its purposefulness."*

Chapter 8 of this book explains the participatory evaluation model, which is one of the most thorough methods of evaluating a program, its goals, and the involvement of people.

The following guidelines are useful for a team before beginning a major evaluation of their work.

Evaluation Guidelines

1. Evaluation shall be carried out in such a way that it is a supportive activity and not a destructive one. Appropriate skills and tools must be used.
2. Evaluation shall be carried out in terms of progress towards goals; from most immediate goals to ultimate goals. Evaluation shall assess whether, in meeting an immediate goal, a broader goal is or is not being achieved.
3. The leadership of the organisations have the authority to require evaluation.
4. All projects and programs of the organisation shall be evaluated at regular intervals.
5. The first one to be heard in all evaluations is the individual or group whose 'work' is being evaluated. But assessment by others, not part of the situation, and/or by those entitled to accountability, is also an integral part of the process.
6. The life of each group within the organisation shall be evaluated at regular intervals.
7. The specific roles of the organisation shall be evaluated at regular intervals.
8. The dignity and respect of people must be honoured and protected in all evaluations.*

b. **Recommendations**

Recommendations include all those items which groups and individuals wish to bring forward as worthy of consideration for acceptance.

Recommendations, written or verbal, from groups or individuals, are considered sacred because they represent the collective effort of the members of the organisation. As such, they are respected and given due consideration by the leadership.

1. MDI Group, Ibid., p. D-5
2. MID Group, Ibid., p.D, 5-8

> ### Clear Procedures for Recommendations
>
> 1. Each member of the organisation (or participant in a program) shall have a clear and easy channel to make suggestions or recommendations.
> 2. All recommendations shall be acknowledged.
> 3. The leadership of the organisation will not lose any written recommendations.
> 4. Members will be helped to develop ideas and recommendations into feasible plans.
> 5. The leadership of the organisation will encourage the members to dream, to plan and to recommend.

c.   **Decision-making**

Helpful guidelines and tools for decision-making have been described in Chapter 7 of this book. It is always a critical point in making something happen.

Decision-making is an expression of the power (collective commitment) of an organisation. A healthy organisation is able to move from one decision to another decision in an orderly and purposeful process.

> ### Decision-making in an Organisation
>
> 1. Decision points (that is, who is responsible for which decisions) shall be clear and understood.
> 2. Decisions shall be made without unnecessary delay.
> 3. Legislative bodies will decide on broad goals and policies, and may confirm broad strategies. They are accountable to the membership.
> 4. Operational decisions are the responsibility of those delegated to do the job.
> 5. Emergency decisions are the responsibility of specific delegated groups or an interim group. Such decisions are confirmed afterwards by the appropriate body.

d.   **Delegation of Responsibilities**

Some of the key problems in implementing decisions and moving to action are:
  — How much should the leader do for the group,
  — How much can (s)he trust the group, and even sometimes,
  — Is the leader actually a bit lazy in helping the group learn new skills, so that next time the group can do the action by themselves?

How often have we heard a leader say, '**it is easier to do it by myself**?' Or how often have we seen a leader going to a Development Office to request things for a group. The long-term consequences of this kind of action is that the group members continue to have no-confidence in themselves as full human beings, and **they feel they have no right to request things themselves that are rightfully theirs**. Dependency on the leader forms a lower self-image in the group.

Learning to delegate responsibility as soon as people can develop the necessary experience and skill is key to fostering their self-reliance and self-respect.

Some **assumptions** about delegation of responsibilities:

1. Delegation is needed whenever a decision is to be implemented. (In most programs no one person can do all the tasks.)
2. Good delegation does not lessen the power of the group or the group leader, but in fact it actually extends the ability of the group and the leader to achieve goals they would be unable to arrive at, either as a whole group, or if the leader worked alone.
3. Commitment grows when people experience taking responsibility. They also need support to balance the risk of trying something new.
4. The delegation process brings out maturity and growth in both parties. It generates commitment, satisfaction and growing interdependence.
    Interdependence is not dependency, nor is it individual isolated action. It is recognition of mutual need for one another.
5. Commitment is often lost if one group abdicates from its responsibility and delegates tasks to another group. Commitment usually builds when responsibility is delegated to small teams or individuals.

Guidelines for Delegating Responsibilities

1. Define what is to be done.
    Give responsibility.
2. Be clear on how well the task is to be done and why. (There is nothing more frustrating than to do a task, like writing a report which you thought was for the members of your small group, only to be told after you have finished it, that it is being sent to the President's office!)
3. Give deadlines and relevant information (or how to find the right information). Also give full access to all resources required for the task.
4. Be clear to others publicly (either in the meeting where the decision is made, or by letter) who has what responsibilities.
5. A time limit must be set for this responsibility. (How many times have we known that a committee or chairperson appointed, has sat in that chair for 10 years!)
6. **Wait for the results.** It is critical not to step in too soon after delegating a responsibility.
7   However, a follow-up system is necessary. Set up a means of communication, either a mid-point report or regularly scheduled meetings. (This is building a support system, and very necessary to give assurance to those taking responsibility. It is also necessary to build accountability.)
8. Thank everyone!

---

3. The Commitment Cycle and Commitment Drain

Individual commitment when it is not caught up in a process leading towards satisfactory implementation of goals, can be drained away and produce many tensions and negative responses. Individuals who have not been helped to come into the program in some useful way will either
— turn their energy against the program,
— set up competing programs, or
— slowly drift away.

One can see in the following diagram how this commitment drain works. If an action has been happening but no real evaluation takes place, as no action is ever perfect, people will become dissatisfied. The dissatisfied people, because their 'grumbling' was not heard in an evaluation either,
— leave the group,
— become angry with the group and turn their energy against the group, or
— they fall out of the program.

Likewise, if the group does have an evaluation but no recommendations are given for changes in the program, or recommendations are ignored, loss of energy and commitment will take place. If recommendations are not turned into concrete decisions, or decisions are made without delegating people to do the job, frustration occurs, and many people drop out. Commitment drains away.

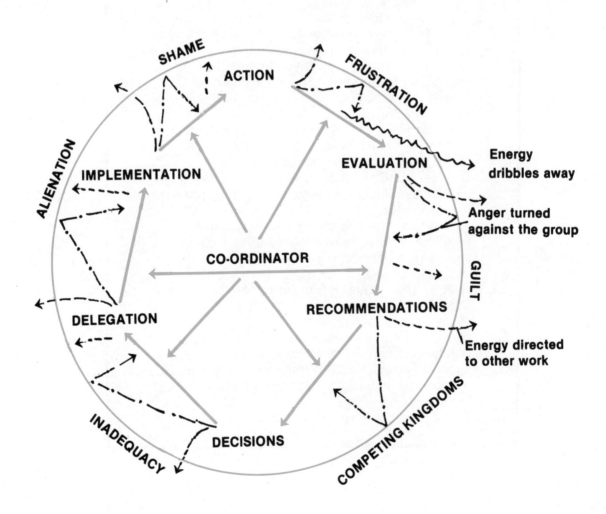

C.   Relationships

In an organisation or movement, people have various expectations of each other. These expectations sometimes are not stated, sometimes they are unconscious. In the rush of activity, an organisation may move along but friction often begins to build up between people. Many times it is because we have different expectations of others and of ourselves in doing a particular task. The following exercises are designs to help clarify roles and expectations between people working together.

1.   ROLE EXPECTATIONS EXERCISE

This is a long but very helpful exercise to sort out the relationships in a group that has been working together on a major task for some time.

Step 1   Ask people to meet in groups with others who carry similar responsibilities. (E.g. priests/sisters/laymen/laywomen or nurses/doctors/administrators/ kitchen staff in a hospital.)
The common goal of the organisation or group should be clearly stated.
Then each group is asked to discuss and write on newsprint:

a.   What do we expect of our own group in accomplishing the task?

b.   What do we expect of each of the other groups in accomplishing the task?

The groups should be no larger than 7 participants. If a group is larger, divide it in half. Both groups will give a presentation. Do not make ambiguous groups or mix functions together.
The groups are given about 1½ hours to do this task. They are then to write their expectations of themselves and of each of the other groups on newsprint. It is best do to this exercise before a natural break. During the break, someone from each group can get all the points written on newsprint.

Step 2   Each group puts their newsprint on the wall and reads out all the points. These points are not elaborated on. After each presentation, participants may ask questions of clarification, but not debate points.

Step 3   After all the groups have presented their expectations, participants are asked to discuss with their neighbour any major conflicts in the expectations of any group that they can see in their presentations. A discussion in the whole group can follow this. This can be a moment of real feedback, so the facilitator should be prepared to help each person hear the others. The facilitator needs to help people not to become defensive and to try to understand why someone may feel the way they do.

Step 4   After this session, there needs to be a break of at least 2 to 3 hours during which a small team can take all the expectations expressed for each group and put these points on one paper. For example, 'What is expected of the nurses by all the other groups' needs to either be re-written on one piece of newsprint or typed on stencils and duplicated for use in the next session.

Step 5 Each group now has a list of expectations from all the other groups in front of them. The homogeneous groups meet again to look at and discuss each point given to them. The group is free to accept or reject any expectation, but they must be able to give their reasons why they cannot fulfil some expectations of them. (For example, one group may request the development staff to be available for any workshops they have. This may be totally unrealistic in terms of the time available by the staff. The staff may respond by saying that they are willing to find appropriate staff for all workshops, if requests are made 3 months in advance.)

Step 6 The whole group comes together and each group responds to the expectations expressed of their group. Comments and discussion can follow each group's response.

Note to facilitator: It is best to introduce the entire exercise with some input and guidelines on Johari's Window and Giving and Receiving Feedback found in Chapter 6 of this book.

Time: The whole exercise takes at least 6 hours. It cannot be rushed because you are dealing with relationships between people. It is sometimes best to spread this exercise over two days.

> **Those who are absent are always wrong.**
> — Congo proverb

2. APPRECIATION—DIFFICULTIES—REQUESTS

The aim of this exercise is to help a group deal effectively with conflicts and tensions which may have been building up for years. The more people's lives overlap, the more inevitable it is that there will be certain areas of conflict. Conflicts and tensions are normal in any group. This is only human. But if conflicts are buried, they can become like infected sores. The group needs to open the sore to let out the conflicts so that healing can be deep and real.

The process of this exercise is similar to that of the previous exercise. The questions given to the homogeneous (similar) groups are different.

Questions

1. What do we appreciate about the other groups (in working in development — or other work)?

2. What do we find difficult in working with the other groups?

3. What would we request from the other groups in future working together?

Again make sure every group reports to the whole group, then has some discussion on the points directed to them, and then every group has a chance to respond to the requests given.

3.   ANALYSING THE STRUCTURE OF AN ORGANISATION

This exercise is most helpful when there are differences of opinion in an organisation about how it should be run (for example, in a women's group the single women, young married women and older women might have different views of how they see the structure and running of the organisation). If the organisation has these conflicts, it usually means it cannot move towards implementing action until the conflict is understood and steps are taken to change the situation.

Procedure

a.   Ask the group to divide into different homogeneous groups (for example, priests, sisters, lay men, women, youth, etc.).

b.   Ask each group to draw on newsprint the way they see the structure of this organisation. Give them a time limit of about 30 minutes to 1 hour.

c.   When they have finished this task, each group presents their picture of the organisation. One person explains the picture for each group.

d.   A discussion in the whole group can follow, on the differences and conflicting viewpoints, or mixed groups of about 3 – 4 people can share their feelings about these differences.

e.   If there are a lot of conflicting ideas, sometimes it is best to leave the discussion here and come back to these drawings half a day later (or after a break).

f.   It is helpful to come back to these conflicts by asking each homogeneous group to look at:
(1)   What can our group do to overcome these conflicts?
(2)   Share these suggestions in the whole group. It is sometimes helpful that each group writes up its suggestions on newsprint.

Time: From 2 – 4 hours.

Materials: Newsprint, felt pens, tape.

Building a movement

In the next chapter, we will deal with the problems of bureaucratic structures. Because many of us have seldom experienced something different than the bureaucratic model, we have difficulty seeing how it can be.

When we are starting a co-operative, or building a political party or establishing basic Christian communities, we often still think in the 'old terms'. We therefore re-establish the old structures for a new task. As Samora Machel has said:

> "Our aim is to build a New Society that corresponds to our interests. Our methods of work must be simple and effective, and our decisions must be *democratic in both form and content*. In content because they correspond to the real interests of the broad masses. In form, because the broad masses participate in drawing up the decisions and feel that they are theirs."*

A movement is one in which membership is open, the structure is participatory and the aims deal with issues which can build solidarity of the majority in society.

---

* *Samora Machel Speaks*, p. 19.

111

A Movement

A Movement
    is dance
       poetry
       music
           which follows no metric
           yet can be precise in capturing reality.

It awakens our soul
       our inner courage
       our reason for being.

It calls us to the Cry
   Demanding our every passion
   tearing down statues built on images of Men
   coming to a kaleidoscope of possibilities which finds a new path
      in search of the Wild Geese.

It beckons us to be released
   defying Norms
   making us laugh at ourselves and
        cry at our fragility.

It asks us to become an Irregular Verb.

It commands us to discipline
   Calling us to attention
         to be at our stations alert,
   tapping our energy and creativity,
         while we willingly give
            our suffering and defeat
            our joy and our laughter
         to the Unknown.

Yet it is like the leaf
   falling from a tree
   caressing us with tenderness.

We are called to
       Dance at the sea
       Dream in the desert and
       Sing on the mountains,
So that we can discover ourselves
       in a New World
           which crumbles old realities
           And refuses to be Named.

It is a battle cry
      yet a song.
Our way of mixing heaven and earth.

                    Sally J. Timmel, January 1980

Chapter 11

New forms of Management and Supervision

·This chapter includes:

Chapter 11

New forms
of Management
and Supervision

Introduction

Most of us have been confined to the western-bureaucratic structures of organisations all of our lives.

We have been taught in bureaucratic schools,
        been sick in bureaucratic hospitals,
        worked in bureaucratic jobs, and
        prayed in bureaucratic churches.

It is difficult to imagine a different model and if we do, we are often called idealistic, utopian and unrealistic. But that is what cultural revolutions have always been about,
      — a change in mentality,
      — a change of structures, and
      — a leap of the imagination.

Society includes a number of institutions (structures), held together by values and ways of doing things (practices) that have become accepted. If a group, a movement or a society has a different vision from the usual values, two areas need to be looked at very seriously:
1. the internal structures of the way in which work is divided, and
2. the nature of work which is not only functional tasks, but creative where each individual needs challenge in order to use his or her capacities.

Current models and practices of management have come from the western or colonial systems whose main purpose has been to maximise profits, increase markets, increase productivity, and thus exploit labour and control workers.

In order to turn this theory upside down and build a human model, we must see that the purpose of management is to enable people (in groups, in communities, and as individuals) to become self-reliant, creative and self-motivating. The term 'management' will need to be replaced by a new term; perhaps 'coordination'. Coordination implies enabling people to
      — reach their own goals,
      — transform their own situation,
      — and take their destiny into their own hands.

As Paulo Freire has said, ''We need to help people to read their reality and write their own history.''

Theory X and Theory Y

Douglas McGregor's theory of management, which he called Theory X and Y, can be a helpful framework to highlight the differences in concepts of management.

McGregor says that there are two theories of management. Both of them deal with the issue of how to organise people. Each theory is based on a certain way of looking at people, an understanding of human nature, and assumptions about motivating and mobilizing people. The two theories have opposite approaches to the problem.

Theory X (Conventional or **Traditional Theory**)

1. Management organises the elements of production (money, materials, equipment, programs and people) for a particular end (in business 'to make profit').
2. People need to be directed, motivated, and controlled.
3. People need to change their behaviour to meet the needs of the organisation.
4. People therefore must be persuaded, rewarded, punished, controlled and supervised very closely.

Beliefs about Human Nature and Theory X

a. The average person is by nature lazy, that is (s)he will work as little as possible if given a chance.
b. The average person lacks ambition, dislikes responsibilities, and prefers to be led.
c. The average person is inherently self-centred, indifferent to organisational needs and goals.
d. The average person is by nature resistant to change.
e. The average person is not very bright and can easily be led by a dictator.

From Theory X the organisation is built like a pyramid with the person(s) at the top controlling the organisation. This is known as 'bureaucracy'. It looks similar to this:

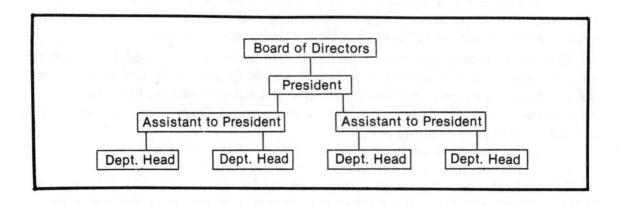

There are many similarities in Theory X to Paulo Freire's description of banking education. Workers in the lower positions of the bureaucracy need to receive instructions passively and silently, doing their required work upon demand.

Top management people give the appearance of great busy-ness, are active with serious decision-making about critical matters, and are aloof, 'above', and superior to other people. Their time is always more 'valuable' than that of those on the bottom of the heap. Top management people are busy giving instruction and developing methods of ensuring that their directives are put into effect. Control and supervision is needed and the second level of management takes on this function.

Theory Y (A New Model)

1. Management can be organised in such a way that decisions can be shared involving all those people who have the knowledge, skill and ability.
2. People are not by nature passive or resistant to organisational needs and goals. They have become so as a result of previous experience in our educational institutions and other organisations.
3. The motivation, ability, capacity for taking responsibility and the readiness to direct one's energies to meet the aims of an organisation are all present in people.
4. 'Managers' are actually co-ordinators to arrange the methods and conditions within the organisation to best achieve the goals.
5. Therefore, the workers' goals are similar to, and linked to the organisational goals.

Beliefs about Human Nature in Theory Y
Beliefs about human nature in Theory Y are just the opposite of Theory X.[1]

The organisation is built on relationships which have similar goals and interests. Decision-making and authority are within different groups of people because of their interest and skills and more often on a horizontal basis rather than top/bottom line. This kind of relational-type organisation might look like this:

a.   for a small organisation   or   b.   a large institution

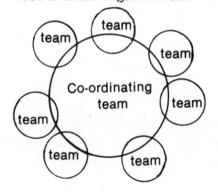
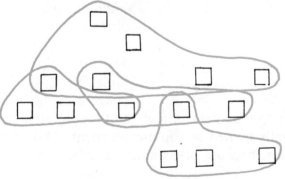

---

1. Adapted from *The Planning of Change*, Bennis, Benne, and Chin. eds. New York: Holt, Rinehart and Winstron, 1969.

As in the **framework of liberating education** as described by Paulo Freire, management is organised for maximum production but with high motivation and responsibility taken by the people. Decisions are taken by the people who are most affected by that decision (for example, workers decide how best to arrange their work in relation to the needs of the country and their own goals for production).[2]

'Managers' or co-ordinators, co-ordinate the work of different groups and help those groups to solve their problems by bringing them together. Discussion and clear sharing of the goals and/or production needs are developed by all the workers. This is seen as not only an educational function but is based on the recognition that **motivation is clearly linked to people's understanding of their relationship to the aims of the organisation.**

If we take Theory X and Y as ultimate choices, we can of course be criticized for over-simplification. However in many institutions, organisations, government ministries and factories, Theory Y can be implemented if there are re-training programmes, effective planning and especially a strong determination and will. Shortcuts and over-concern for efficiency and immediate results, only short-circuit a very critical area of implementing the type of human society we are aiming at.

"**The long march through the institutions**" as Marcuse has said, is often **the very step missing** in building the socialism one aspires to.

Theory X and Y — Discussion Questions

1. Consider one of the organisations you know well. In what way does it reflect Theory X structures and attitudes?
2. Do you think it would be possible and desirable to move towards Theory Y? If so, why? If not, why not?
3. What steps would be necessary in order to start a move towards Theory Y?

The Bureaucratic Structure

Different organisations and groups, or different government ministries need different styles of management **based on the aims and needs of that organisation.** Obviously the Ministry of Defence and the Ministry of Community Development need quite different approaches to management because their aims and functions are different.

A charity organisation whose aim is distribution of food during a famine, and another one whose aim is community education, again each must have different structures and practices of management.

The bureaucratic structure, is by its very nature, one in which:
- communication,
- planning,
- problem-solving,
- decision-making,
- supervision,
- image-making,

are in the hands of a few and thus the structure of an institution or organisation is virtually owned by top management. This ultimately leads to great social divisions, whether because of economic strata, social position, or political power.

---

2. See *Self-Management, Economic Liberation of Man.* Edited by Jaroslav Vanek. Penguin Books, Baltimore, Maryland, 1975, for elaboration of this point.

Practices in a Bureaucracy

Communication in a bureaucracy is usually top down. Although in recent years there has been a move to consult workers or lower-level staff, top management still has control of what they will implement. This method of consulting is seen by top management as a way to make the organisation or business run more efficiently. Another purpose is to give workers the illusion of participation.

Planning is usually done at the top. Meetings between top officials continue and take up most people's time. They plan 'for' others.

Problem-solving is one of the main tasks of top management. Problems at the bottom are passed-up the ladder for solutions. People at the bottom are not encouraged to think or to take responsibility. Information is not shared at different levels.

Decisions are therefore taken by people on top. People at the bottom fear taking decisions either because what they decide could be vetoed by someone above them, or that they will be seen as 'stepping out of line'.

As power, decision-making, planning and authority is located at the top of an organisation, one can see how top managers begin using language indicative of **ownership**; 'my school', 'my church', 'my ministry'. Even in service organisations, ownership can be found by top managers.

Supervision often can mean inspection. It is often a function of control over the workers, and not one of enabling the workers or staff to produce their maximum efforts.

Image-making is very necessary in a bureaucratic organisation because the people do not feel that they own that organisation. It is not theirs, it is not a part of them. So managers go around trying to 'sell' themselves, their organisation, their 'product'.

When real needs are not being met by an organisation, then it is necessary to persuade people.

Sell the product.
Sell the idea.
People are consumers.
People will eat anything.
People can be manipulated.
People are not critical.

Results of Bureaucracy on People's Level of Awareness

In a bureaucracy, people accept their position, and often see the only way out is to climb the ladder. **Individuals are isolated and separated** from others. They are a part of a machine. Look at most of the office buildings and see how the long corridors, individual rooms with doors closed, and intermediary bodies (called messengers) promote this isolation.

Through rewards and a possible chance of promotion, the system teaches that competition is necessary. Competition is valued because it is supposed to keep up individual initiative. We have learned this very well in school. The results are that we must step on our brothers and sisters in order that we can get on top.

To climb to the top becomes the central meaning for many people in their lives. This produces **individualism.** This individualism separates people from a communal sense of responsibility. Everyone is looking out for themselves. Even if one would like to promote more social responsibility, a sense of powerlessness is experienced. "What can one person do?" becomes a common cry.

Although there is an extreme degree of isolation and individualism which is promoted in the bureaucratic management, there is also a strong conformity to the values and practices that exist in an organisation. People will agree that each one must stay in their 'place'. This division is a way to make sure that secretaries will not identify with messengers, that teachers will not identify with secretaries, that headmasters will not identify with teachers and so on. Thus a co-operative approach to tackling the essential problems of that organisation is completely blocked.

This method has been notoriously illustrated by the colonial administrations of 'divide and rule'.

> "The oppressor in a desperate bid to maintain the status quo, resorts to unrestrained guile and craft, to frighten, demoralise, divide and confuse the oppressed. He will ensure the obliteration of all vestiges of self-confidence in the spirit of the oppressed poor, resulting in the latter's succumbing to a defeatism that shies away from any conflict, verbal or physical with the oppressor. As the poor nearly exploding with tension, seek to ventilate their frustration, the oppressor deflects their wrath from himself by what Frantz Fanon calls 'Horizontal violence" — studiously staged violence between the oppressed themselves. He will foster ugly division and splits against the people's unity of purpose. More and more the leaders of the poor will be tempted by the prospect of immediate personal gain at the expense of the people.
>
> This is the problem of elitism. An elite is created on the basis of education and economic considerations, and used as a buffer between the oppressor and the oppressed. The legitimate aspirations of the poor remain unsatisfied. No change has taken place except in the oppressing family which has become an extended family. Elitism has been substituted for racism. But the tragic effects on the poor are the same if not worse."
>
> Canaan Banana
> **The Gospel According to the Ghetto**, p. 69.

One of the main reasons for division of labour is **strict control over people**, making sure no unity of ideas or class interests are formed.

These divisions:

— economically (large differences of salaries),
— socially (by rank, prestige, and position),
— politically (concentration of power), and
— ideologically (people at all levels always reaching to climb another step up the ladder, and becoming resistant to the search for changes),

all alienate people from the core of life,

from work,
from productivity,
from service, and
from social concern for their neighbours.

This fundamental social structure within any institution is of course one of the most difficult areas to transform since the very people 'who are on top' will usually not make such changes because it is against their own self-interest.

This top dog position and attitude which comes from the bureaucratic structure, has an effect all through society. The following cartoons illustrate this well.

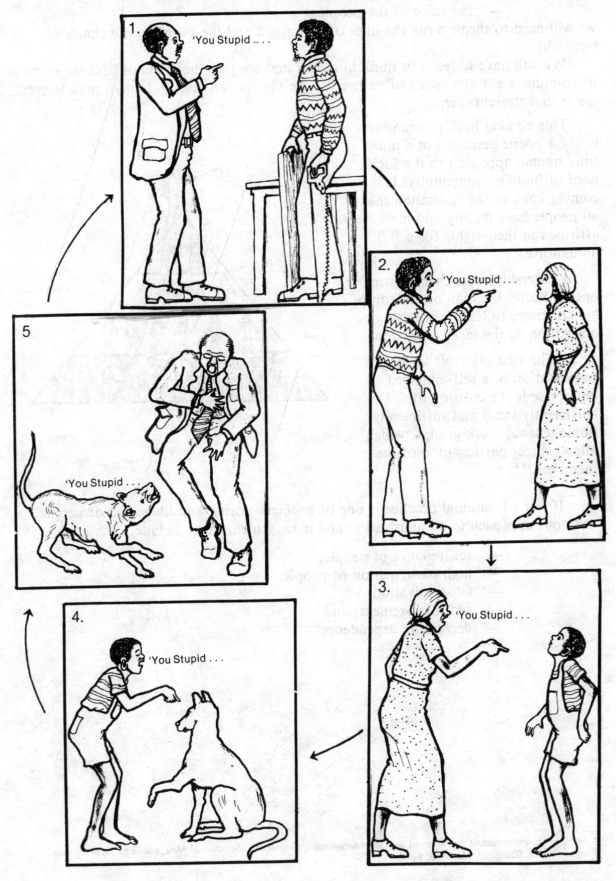

What Could be a New Model of Management?

To think out and to implement a new form of management which takes into account:

— the needs of the people,
— the dignity of people, and
— the voice of the people,

we will need to throw away the lines of command and the bureaucratic charts of hierarchy.

We will have to learn to think in circles and see the wholeness of life: the earth in its roundness and the cycles of nature. As we always can see, no human path is ever made in a straight line.

This coming back to roundness is not a poetic gesture, but a more fully human approach to the social need of building community. It is coming back to the realisation that all people have dignity and must be affirmed in their rights for a full human life.

Leadership must change from one authoritarian man on the top of his kingdom, to team work and co-ordination of the tasks to be done.

"The first principle in the organisation of a self-managed enterprise is the creation of sufficiently small and sufficiently homogeneous work groups, which allows direct participation of the members."*

If our educational practice is one of problem-posing and liberation of people, then our approach to administration and management must include:

— self-reliance of people,
— high participation of people,
— self-motivation,
— self-management, and
— decreasing dependency.

---

* For a fuller description of a new model see, *Self-Management, Economic Liberation of Man*, edited by Jaroslav Vanek, Penguin Books, Baltimore, Md. 1975, Pg. 141

The Structure

Structures must be flexible with small units taking full responsibility for their work. It would look something like this:

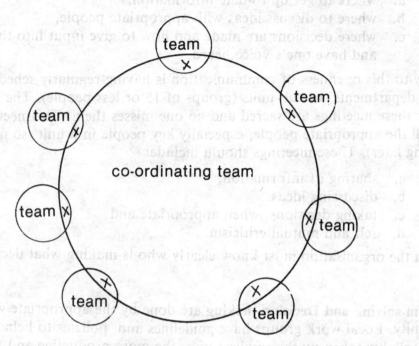

One can enlarge upon this simple diagram to fit the size and complexity of an organisation, but the basic principle is team work with people accountable to each other in the appropriate areas of work. Regional or local teams are accountable to the people they serve on a political level. They are also accountable and responsible for the task they do on a professional level, to a co-ordinating group.

For a more complete understanding on how to train people for team-management and the development of enabling structures, see Chapter 10 in this book.

Practices of Enabling Management

A manager becomes a co-ordinator. Co-ordination involves both relationships between people and events. The role of the co-ordinator is to help place people in such a way that they can develop good relationships with each other so that work can be carried out effectively.

A co-ordinator is to help support, build and challenge the actions of groups, not to foster competition or dependency. The co-ordinator helps to build teams and groups so that they themselves become self-directing, self-starting, self-controlling, and self-managing. Creativity and taking initiative on the local levels are encouraged.

Communication is based on dialogue. Those most affected and directly related to a task take responsibility for that work. Orders are never given. Work is seen as a mutual task to be done and a mutual learning process.

The important principle is to **have clear, transparent and open forms of communications** which everyone in the organisation knows about. Informal or underground patterns of communication can lead to

- nepotism,
- brotherisation,
- sexual harrassment,
- corruption,
- unequal access to power, and
  individualistic influences.

In the book *Self-Management*, the term **transparency** is used to describe the decision-making structure in Yugoslavia. What this means in practice is that people know:

    a.   where to get up-to-date information,
    b.   where to discuss ideas with appropriate people,
    c.   where decisions are made and how to give input into that process and have one's voice heard.

The key to this openness of communication is having regularly scheduled meetings of departments, or sub-units (groups of 15 or less people). The regular hours set aside for these meetings are sacred and no one misses them! The meetings should consist of all the appropriate people, especially key people in a unit (so no one can veto anything later). These meetings should include:

    a.   sharing of information,
    b.   discussing ideas,
    c.   taking decisions, when appropriate and
    d.   self and mutual criticism.

Everyone in the organisation must know clearly who is making what decisions, when and where.

Problem-solving and Decision-making are done by the appropriate work group or the community. Local work groups have guidelines and policies to help them, but the more responsibility taken by the smallest unit, the more productive and the more self-managing the community can become.

The way a group works is decided by that group itself. **They decide their own procedures based on the goals** and direction of the organisation, their particular area of work, and on their strengths and weaknesses. Work teams decide their own hours of work in relation to other units and in relation to the whole organisation. Flexible hours in fact have proved more efficient than the '9 to 5' syndrome set down by the bureaucratic model.

Family responsibilities are taken into account rather than hidden. How many times have we seen the 'jacket on the back of an office chair' and the person out on family matters. Many studies have shown that when people share responsibility for their work in a team, efficiency and productivity improves.*

Peers and co-workers have demonstrated that they give more accountability to each other than they do to 'top management'. Increased production occurs more from pressure from one's co-workers than because of higher salaries or directives.

But not everyone needs to decide how many paper clips to order! How often have we sat in meetings and been bored because the group was asked to make decisions on details. It is a sure way to lose commitment.

> **Becoming overly democratic in the end produces less democracy.**

* Amitai Etzioni, *Modern Organisations,* Prentice-Hall, Inc. Englewood Cliffs, New Jersey, USA, 1964, pp. 32—37.

In general, many people need to be involved in the broad areas of the life of an organisation, such as the aims, vision, goals, policies, recommendation and evaluation. Other tasks become the responsibility of smaller units. A guideline would look like this:

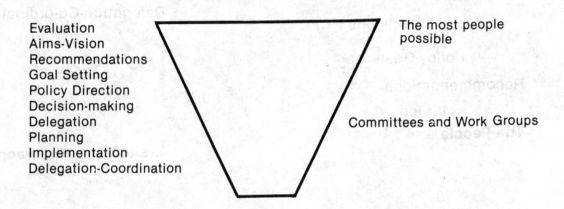

Evaluation
Aims-Vision
Recommendations
Goal Setting
Policy Direction
Decision-making
Delegation
Planning
Implementation
Delegation-Coordination

The most people possible

Committees and Work Groups

You will notice the above diagram is the opposite of the usual bureaucratic model.

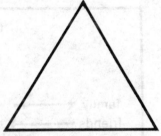

Planning includes many levels of participation from people. As much as possible, people need to be involved in several levels:

— defining the needs,
— sharing in the formulation of the aims,
— making recommendations and
— evaluation.

The general direction and policy development comes from the people. From there, the recommendations are summarised and given to a representative decision-making body. At this point, the implementation of decisions is a matter of expertise and not a democratic procedure. That is, a farmer does not sit on the committee to re-design the physics syllabus related to factories. The English teacher does not sit on the committee to develop a rural women's preventive health care program.

As in Yugoslavia, this process **separates political authority from professional authority**. These two kinds of authority need to be respected, understood and seen clearly within the structure.

> Political authority comes from the people. Professional authority comes from the people who have specific skills, experience and interest.

As seen in the Parabola model in Chapter 10, this distinction would look like this:

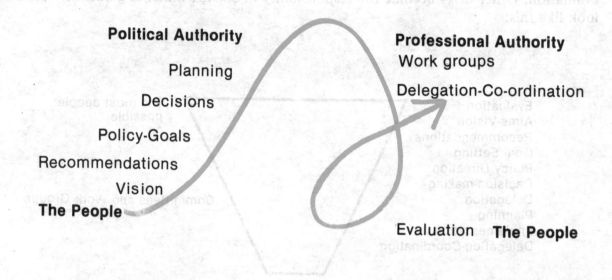

Political Authority

Planning

Decisions

Policy-Goals

Recommendations

Vision

The People

Professional Authority
Work groups

Delegation-Co-ordination

Evaluation **The People**

Supervision is done through regular evaluations and through the process of self and mutual criticism. Corruption and low production can easily happen in any structure.

Accountability needs to be seen on many levels. Team members are responsible to those nearest them, but also to the wider society, as seen in the diagram. Through regular evaluations, each person can learn new skills and constructive ways of change.

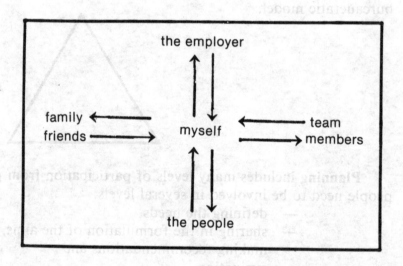

Helping people to develop a critical awareness of their own situation is a vital link to changing structures. If a people have been submissive, passive and dominated for generations, their ability to welcome change and even to imagine that it can happen will be slow and hesitant.

Practice is important. Participation includes the power to take one's destiny in one's own hands, which means making decisions. Through an enabling management style, we can foster people's ability to change their situation.

126

People's Power

The creation of the People's Assemblies means the consolidation of class power, of people's power. This is an important moment when the people in an organised way affirm the reality of their power. The power of the people serves the people; strengthening it improves the people's lives. . . .

The question of power is fundamental to the revolution. The revolution triumphs or fails when it holds or loses power. According to bourgeois theorists the state is neutral. . .

We found that we must prevent Mozambican exploiters from occupying the vacancies left by colonialism, prevent the small national exploiters allied to imperialism from occupying power and progressively turning themselves into a new bourgeoisie. Our fight was to destroy the small crocodile on the river bank instead of leaving him to grow and turn into a strong crocodile. We did this by destroying the political and economic power of the feudal chiefs; we also did it when we took control of trade and encouraged the organisation of collective modes of production in the liberated areas. As far

as structures were concerned we systematically rejected all those who aspired to become new exploiters. The people's committees of peasants in cooperatives and poor peasants, allied to the soldiers, were the first forms the new power in liberated areas.

Samora Machel Speaks
pp. 4 – 6.

Administration and Management Codes and Exercises

The following codes, exercises and guided discussions can be useful to help people re-examine their beliefs and style of management. They can also be helpful to people who need more skills in this area.

1.   CORRUPTION CODE

The aim of this play is to help people reflect on some aspects of corruption that happen in society and how they can either find ways to stop it or ways that they themselves will not become part of it.

The Play

Three people are needed for this play. One person is a young woman who is newly appointed as the Social Welfare Officer. She is alone in the office, coming about 10 minutes late. She is sitting reading her newspaper and talking to herself. She thinks she needs more money and is finding it difficult to find ways to earn more.

A young man who has been the Youth Officer comes in and goes to his desk. He asks her about her troubles. He starts to tell her how easy it is to get money, like how he found a friend to give false vouchers at a hotel. He starts to give her advice on how to sell blankets that are in the storeroom.

At this point the Community Development Officer comes in, greets his workers and goes into his private office. He gets on the telephone to a man he met at the bar the previous night. He works out a deal for large amounts of money on a particular project.

This play can be elaborated, but the focus should mainly be on money and corruption, with the small additions about being late for work and doing personal business on work time.

Discussion Questions

These questions can be discussed in small groups of 3's and then shared in the whole group.
1.   What happened in the play?
2.   What are the reasons for this kind of mentality?
3.   What are the main values presented in the play?
4.   Are these the same values in our society today?
     How are they similar or different?
5.   Can church workers and church projects be different from others in society? Realistically — how can this be done?
6.   What is our responsibility if we see others practising corruption?
     (This last question is best to discuss in local teams and using very specific cases.)

2. PERSONAL AND PUBLIC FUNDS

This exercise is to help people reflect on how their own use of personal money and their planning of their own budgets can affect their work. This can lead to a discussion on how one's personal financial situation can affect our attitudes towards public funds.

Procedure

a. The following self-questionnaire is given out to everyone. Emphasise that this is a private questionnaire.

Questionnaire

This questionnaire is for your own use. **Do NOT** show it to anyone unless you wish to. We will refer to it only in general in the discussion.

_____ 1. Do you have a current account (cheque account)?

_____ 2. Does it have a balance in it today?

_____ 3. Do you have a savings account?

_____ 4. If so, how much do you put in it each month (on an average)?

_____ 5. Do you have a farm or plot of land?

_____ 6. If so, how much do you spend to improve it each month?

_____ 7. Do you give money regularly to relatives?

_____ 8. Do you give loans to others?

_____ 9. Do you need to receive loans from others sometimes?

_____ 10. How much of your time is spent on personal finances per month (that is, seeing friends, relatives, banks, etc.)?

_____ 11. How much monthly demands are made on you for contributions to projects and other things?

---

b. After everyone has finished answering these questions, the following statement is put up on newsprint:

"If your answers to numbers 2, 4, and 6 were low or Nil and if your answers to 7, 8, and 9 were YES, you should not be a manager or worker in a church project."

"Do you agree or disagree with this statement? Why or why not?"

c. Read these statements to the group. It can be useful to have them discuss these in small group of similar backgrounds, like all women, etc.

d. The discussion in the whole group, after the small groups, can be very intense. There is no real 'right' or 'wrong' answer to the question. It is a question of self-examination. How much do the pressures that are put on people lead them to be tempted to use the money from a project?

The integrity, reliability and accountability of the people involved in projects will determine the future of the projects involved.

Summary

A good summary following these two exercises can be the short input called. "Practical Projects: A Help or a Hindrance to Transformation" found in Chapter 3, pages 91 and 92.

3. A CASE STUDY OF GROUP ACCOUNTS

The following case study can be used to help groups look at the need for keeping clear accounts which all the members can understand.

The Case Study*

The Nyakongo Women's Group has 25 members. They have three office bearers: a chairperson, secretary and treasurer. Members paid a $5 annual contribution of which $3 was given to a church fund.

They have the following activities:

- agriculture — a vegetable garden,
- handicrafts — sewing of tablecloths and making palm leaf baskets,
- fund raising — each member contributes $1 per meeting.

The group meets once a week. In order to develop their garden, the Women's Group took a loan from the church Savings and Credit Society for ploughing. The first loan was for $80. A second loan was for $50. There was also a loan given to them of seeds including:

- 1 bag of maize worth $10,
- 1 bag of sunflower seeds worth $12.

The loans were given for 6 months.

They harvested:

- 6 bags of sunflowers of 40 Kg. for which they received $15 for each bag,
- 8 bags of maize which they sold at the local market.

A meeting was called by the chairperson to discuss the distribution of the profits made. The income from the palm leaf baskets and tablecloths was $150. They had spent $75 on materials.

The secretary reported to the meeting how much money was collected from the sales. The treasurer was not present at the meeting to answer questions from the members. Three tins of maize were not accounted for and some members claimed that these were sold by the treasurer to the local beerhall after agreement with the chairperson. The chairperson denied this. The secretary tried to argue with the women not to let this issue spoil the meeting.

Members asked the secretary to divide all the money earned by the members. The secretary however claimed to have no records of who came to work, how often they came, and how much money they received for the baskets and tablecloths which were sold.

Members now really started accusing their office bearers of mis-using the trust given to them, and started asking where all their money had gone.

Members were asked to come back in a week's time to discuss the same agenda.

---

* Developed by Ria van Iersel, Ahero, Kenya, 1976.

Discussion Questions

1. What are the causes of the problems in Nyakongo?
2. What immediate action is needed?
3. What is needed to prevent similar situations in the future?
   What structures are needed?
   Who needs to be involved?
4. What should be the specific responsibilities of:
   a. the chairperson?
   b. secretary?
   c. treasurer?
5. What are the responsibilities of the members?

Procedure

a. Ask people to discuss this case study in small groups. Usually it is helpful if everyone has a copy of the case study and then it is read out loud in the whole group before small group discussions.

b. In the whole group, share ideas on each question and put on newsprint, their answers to questions 3 and 4. Reflect on these answers in relation to their own group.

c. **Practice session on simple accounts**

An outline of how to set up accounts can then be explained. One can use the above case study and demonstrate on a blackboard the following method:

IN

Membership:	25 × $5	= $125.00
Fund raising:	$480	= 480.00
Loans:	$ 80.00	= 152.00
	$ 50.00	
	$ 10.00	
	$ 12.00	
Sales: Sunflowers		= 90.00
Maize		= 160.00
Handicraft		= 150.00

Total Income: = 1,157.00

OUT

Diocesan Fund 25 × $3	=	$75.00
Loans	=	152.00
Materials	=	75.00

Total Expenses = 302.00

Balance carried forward: $855.00

4. SIMPLE ACCOUNTS: A SKILL PRACTICE

The following case study is given to each participant as a handout.

Village Case Study

September

1.9.82	Mr. John Kato and Robert Maya, group members, contribute $20 each.
12.9.82	A grant of $1,500 is received from Oxfam to buy materials for the village water project.
23.9.82	Anne Dudu and Teresa Kali, group members, contribute $20 each.
24.9.82	A grant of $600 is given to group from the diocesan development office. It can be used for loans only, of no more than $50 per person for purchase of farm tools.
27.9.82	Mike Mulwa and Patrick Mataka receive loans of $50 each.
29.9.82	10 bags of cement are bought by the group at $60 each.

October

3.10.82	A local mason is paid $50 for work done on the group building.
5.10.82	Loan of $20 given to Nyaga.
5.10.82	Mike Mulwa repays $15 for his loan.
7.10.82	Loan given to Wanjiro of $25.
18.10.82	$45 paid to people for breaking stones.
23.10.82	$23 paid for sodas, tea, etc. for a party given in honour of a local chief.

November

3.11.82	Mike Mulwa repays $20 for his loan.
3.11.82	Patrick Mataka repays $25 for his loan.
5.11.82	Nyaga repays $10 for his loan.
6.11.82	Cement and iron bars bought at the cost of $120.
6.11.82	Plough and seeds bought for a widow at $60.
28.11.82	Widow pays back $5 to the group.

Procedure

a. Ask each participant to record the amount of cash received (income), and the amount of cash given out (expenses). If possible, they should do this on regular bookkeeping journal paper.

b. After they finish, show them on the blackboard or on a piece of newsprint, the correct accounts.

c. Ask each participant to find their errors and correct them. Slowly go around to each participant and see what problems they had.

d. Give time for questions and answers, and give simple instructions for any general mistakes the group is making. Following handout can be given to each participant.

Time: About 1 hour, but depends on the experience of the participants.

Materials: Copies of the Village Case Study for each participant and two pages of regular bookkeeping journal paper for each participant. Pencils.

Keeping a Project Account

What we are basically interested in when keeping accounts is that any person can see very clearly where the project cash has come from, and where and how the project cash was spent.

Two Golden Rules
a. Every cash you receive, make a receipt for it.
b. For every cash spent, make a voucher for it with someone's authority.

When spending cash, always make sure that you have got authority from the persons who are responsible and make sure that person(s) signs before you pay out the cash. Make the receiver sign before taking the cash or put a thumbmark.

Why do we do this?

First, it is very easy to forget where money has come from and where it is going. When you are recording the accounts in the books, if you have not had this system, your accounts will not balance. Thus it is much better to take the time, on the spot, to give receipts and make out vouchers. Doing it later means you most likely forget.

The second reason is a question of honesty and accountability. You are responsible for a group's money — this is not your money. If these account books are kept up-to-date, any member of the group, any outside person, and any person in authority can see very quickly where the money has gone.

Because money can lead to great distrust, the person who handles it must prove they are trustworthy. One should not think others are not trusting us if they want to see receipts. The burden of proof is on the person who receives and uses cash.

After keeping an account of all money received and all money spent, you then record all items into a cash book at the end of each month.

Financial Reports

When you are reporting your finances to a group, these three points should be kept in mind:
a. state very clearly the income and expenses,
b. state whether a profit was made or if there is a deficit (or in other words, the balance).
c. If some people have failed to pay back a loan, explain that in your statement of accounts.

5.   A CASE STUDY: LOANS TO GROUPS*

The following letter can be used as a code, followed by a discussion in groups.

Mr. John Awiti   Oritu 1.8.1984
Parish Council Chairman
X Mission, P.O. Barata

Dear Mr. Awiti:
   I am glad to inform you that our Youth Program got off the ground
and after the four weeks training, the youth leaders have got down to
work with great enthusiasm.
   Many Parish Youth Clubs have been formed and a revolving fund
was started to support initiatives taken by small groups of 5 – 10 young
people who have no employment. They are to work together and start
something so as to be self-employed.
   The Youth Co-ordinator visits the clubs to discuss the purpose of
the revolving fund and to discuss the projects.
   In one of our Youth Clubs, something went wrong which is
threatening the life of the club. Some leaders have made themselves
members of a few loan groups. Some of their names appear in five
different requests. Some young teachers have also applied for loans from
the revolving fund. Obviously they do not qualify for the loan because
they are employed, but they are also on the parish council.
   I know that you are very highly respected in our parish and
sometimes it can be helpful to have someone who knows the people,
come to help us through our problems. I also worry that this kind of
situation could spread to other groups. Since you are also on the
regional council, we are wondering if you can help us.

                                                        Yours sincerely,
                                                        Joseph Okondo

---

Discussion Questions

1. What led to this situation?
2. What could happen to the Parish Youth Club?
3. What immediate action is needed?
4. What is needed to prevent similar situations like this in the future?

Summary

During the above discussion, it can be helpful to raise questions about the purpose and the need of revolving funds. The usual aim of a revolving fund is to help people who are in need, not to give individual loans to those who have. It is an initial push to a group to begin a project and to build unity. With the loan being a revolving system, it helps the groups to become aware of the needs of other groups. It is important to make clear that other groups who are very much in need are dependent on each group paying back their loan on time.

---

* Developed by Jeremias Carvalho, Meru, Kenya, 1979.

In order for a revolving loan system to be effective, several precautions need to be taken in order to lessen the chances of default. These include:

a. **Clarity.**   The aims of the group must be clear. The procedures, policies and practices about loans must be clear to every member:
  — who is entitled to a loan,
  — how much,
  — when it has to be paid back, etc.

b. **Awareness.** Both the group and the community need to know about the loan, but also some education about the purpose and aims is needed. This public knowledge of the loans and purpose, helps to be a kind of social pressure for the group not to let the community down.

c. **Book-keeping and Supervision.**   This is very important so that people are accountable for funds.

d. **Immediate follow-up** is essential instead of waiting until a project is near to failure or the money has disappeared.

Time: 1 – 1½ hours.

Materials: Copies of the case study for each participant.

6.   REPORT WRITING

Give the following guidelines to the group.

```
                    Guidelines for Writing a Report*

       The following points need to be kept in mind when writing a report.

   a.  THINK.     For whom are you writing the report?
                  What do they want to know?
                  Why do they want to know it?
                  What do you want to say?

   b.  WRITE      (i)   A Narrative describing the project or the program.
                        The content, process, atmosphere.
                  (ii)  Statistics (numbers of people or ploughs) and
                        finances.
                  (iii) Evaluation of Project — from the participants and
                        others.
                  (iv)  Project. From the evaluation, what is the expected,
                        growth, changes or development of the project?

   c.  CHECK      Is the content clear?
                  Is it true?
                  Does it convey the atmosphere?
                  Does it express the process?
```

* Developed by Fr. Paddy O'Reilly, Kitui, Kenya, 1979.

Exercise

After the input on how to write a report, participants are asked to write a report of the present workshop for some group back home. They are given one hour to do this. When they have finished, each participant finds another participant to check their report. It can be very useful if the animators would also check the reports and give a critique.

Time: 1½ – 2 hours.

Materials: Paper, pens, and input ready.

7. WRITING SIMPLE PROPOSALS

In order to write a good proposal for a project, one must first have a good project. No matter how simple the project, one must be able to demonstrate that it is worthy of support. The group must know what it is aiming at, and have a concrete plan on how to achieve those aims. Many times it is not possible to present a project verbally to a funding group. It is therefore very important to be able to write a simple proposal.

The following guidelines are important for a group to consider before writing a proposal.

Guidelines for a Project

a. Does it help to meet **basic needs**, especially of the poorest people?
b. Does it use **local resources**? Does it build skills for the future?
c. Does it show a move towards **self-reliance**? Does it reduce the dependence on outside resources?
d. Does it build upon good local **cultural** patterns? Are people really involved?
e. Does it make the life of the people more fulfilled? Is there **human enrichment**?
f. Does the project spoil or **improve the environment**? (e.g. soil erosion)

A group needs to consider these points before applying for funds. When these questions are answered, then a smaller group needs to write a simple proposal. The group needs to be aware that because they have written a proposal, it does not mean that they will get funds. It must be prepared for feedback and even changing its project.

A general outline for writing a simple proposal

a. What is the name of the project?
b. To whom are you sending the proposal?
c. Who will be legally responsible for the money?
   What is your structure of accountability?
d. What is the problem that this project is trying to deal with?
   Give background information about the area, people, etc.
e. What specific group or groups are involved?
f. What is the plan of the project and how will it help solve the problem?

g.   What resources will be required?
      What is needed locally?
      What is needed from outside and why is this not available locally?
      How is this project coordinated with other projects in the area;
      the government, other churches, or other groups?

h.   What is the time plan for implementation?
      When will it begin?
      How long will the project take?
      When will it finish?
      How many people finally will be involved?

i.   What person or team will be responsible for the project? How have they
      demonstrated that they are capable of running the project?

j.   What are the plans to make the project self-reliant?

k.   What are the estimated costs of the project?
      How much local contribution is expected?
      How much are you asking from the funding group?

l.   How would you like payments?
      What is the name of the group's bank account?

m.   Give date and signatures of the appropriate people in the project.

8.   TEAM MANAGEMENT: AN EXERCISE

As we are planning actions as a
team, we are in fact developing
some kind of organisation (whether
it is formal or non-formal). If
leaders are using the Problem-
Posing approach to community
development, the type of
organisation that develops must also
have similar aims and a structure
which does not oppose the basic
principles of the problem-posing
method.

The following elements of an organisation will have to be considered:

Guidelines for a more Human Organisation

a.   It creates an open and problem-solving climate.
b.   Decision-making includes the people most directly affected.
c.   It builds trust among individuals and groups.
d.   It reduces unhealthy competition and maximizes co-operative efforts.
e.   It reduces social and class distinctions equalizing manual and intellectual work by all its members.
f.   It develops a procedure which recognizes both the achievement of the aim and the growth of people.
g.   It promotes self-discipline, self-direction, and self-reliance of its members.
h.   It moves to shared leadership and authority.

Exercise

1.   Give copies of the following questionnaire to each member of the team or group. Ask each person to answer the questions and then as a group, discuss any differences they discover in their answers.

2.   If there are some problems between members, the team should try to solve the problems.

Time: 45 minutes to 1½ hours.

Materials: One copy of each questionnaire for each participant.

Where are you in your Organisation?*

A Questionnaire

Organisation Process	Description	Reaction (Check 1 item per box)
INFLUENCE	How much of a say do you have in determining the organisation's actions and directions?	☐ enough ☐ not enough
STRUCTURE	How do you feel about the structure of the organisation?	☐ it's too tight, rigid, controlling ☐ just right ☐ too loose
RESOURCES	How well do you feel your resources (skills, interests, abilities) are being used?	☐ I'm over-used ☐ used just right ☐ I'm under-used
EXPERIMENTATION	How creative, experimental, risk-taking, is the organisation?	☐ Not enough ☐ just right ☐ too conservative
INTERGROUP COMMUNICATION	How much communication is there between you and other units in the organisation?	☐ too much ☐ just enough ☐ not enough
GOALS	How challenging are the goals of the organisation right now?	☐ too challenging and demanding ☐ just right ☐ too simple and undemanding
INVOLVEMENT	How involved and interested are you in the organisation's activities	☐ very involved ☐ just right ☐ uninvolved
TIME	How do you feel about the amount of time you have for the work?	☐ too much time ☐ just right ☐ not enough time
LEARNING	How good an experience is this for your learning about how organisations work?	☐ very good ☐ good ☐ fair ☐ poor ☐ very poor

---

* Episcopal Church, *Basic Reader in Human Relations Training*, Part VI, p. 178.

9.   A CHALLENGE TO ORGANISE

The aim of this exercise is to look at three areas of problems that arise in developing an organisation:

a. Our own personal **style of leadership** and the effects of our leadership on a group;

b. Satisfaction with **decision-making** within a group. How does decision-making affect behaviour of group members?

c. Various ways of **developing an organisation to meet the needs** of a group.

Procedure

a. The following task is given to the group early in the afternoon.

b. **The task**
"You are to plan a supper and an evening program which will give a high degree of satisfaction to all the members of this group. You may use the kitchen and the dining room and spend up to $1.00 per person. The normal kitchen staff have been given a free afternoon and evening. The training staff will participate in the evening program but not in the preparation except as consultants if necessary. The program should start at 6.30 p.m. and finish at 9 p.m."

c. It can help the final discussion if in the middle of the task and at the end, the group is asked to answer the following questions individually:

   (i) How involved do you feel in the task?
      ☐ Very involved
      ☐ Fairly involved
      ☐ Not involved
      ☐ Very bored

   (ii) How satisfied are you with the way in which this group is making decisions?
      ☐ Very satisfied
      ☐ Satisfied
      ☐ Dissatisfied
      ☐ Very dissatisfied.

   (iii) Write down 3 adjectives that describe for you the atmosphere of the group now.

d. When the program is completed at 9 p.m., the staff can ask the same questions again and tabulate the differences.

e. The next morning the animators can use the following questions to guide the reflection on the experience.

Discussion Questions

a. What helped and what hindered our decision-making?

b. How did we feel when our own suggestions (or our own desires) were not taken seriously by the group?

c. Who had the most influence in the group? Did we find this helpful or not helpful? Why?

d. What kind of an organisation did we develop? Describe and draw a diagram. On what basis did we form work teams?

e. What helped each member to feel productive in doing the tasks? What hindered? Was there a need for more or less structure to help members become more productive to the group?

f. How did you feel about the structure which developed? What have you learnt about appropriate structures to get a task done, to provide work satisfaction for those involved?

Summary

This exercise is rich in giving a group a common experience to analyse. It is possible to divide the discussion questions into the three areas and have short theories after each of the discussions.

a. Leadership theories can be found in Chapter 10

b. Decision-making theories can be found in Chapter 7

Theory X and Theory Y found at the beginning of this chapter is useful to look at different structures of an organisation.

Time: A minimum of one day.

Materials: Use of a kitchen, money to buy food, reaction forms for the mid-point and final evaluation, newsprint, tape and felt pens.

SUPERVISION

Codes and Exercises for Supervision*

**A supervisor is a counselor; someone who enables others to
solve their problems and become self-reliant.**

Supervision, in some instances, has come to mean 'inspection' . This would mean
one would train people to quantify what they see, hear and observe. How many
people attend a class? How much material did a teacher cover in a syllabus? How
many students passed a certain examination?

However, for those people involved in problem-posing and learner-centred
education, supervision takes on a totally new function. The role of the supervisor is
that of a counsellor.

Counselling skills deal with human relations. These include:
— entering into problem-solving with people,
— learning to be sensitive to others on a very deep and personal level,
— diagnosing problems within a group,
— enabling people to solve their own problems,
— challenging people in a way which can be accepted,
— helping people to deal with conflict, and
— learning to listen creatively.

Learning some of these counselling skills is of course a long-term process which
many people take years to study. However, it can be helpful to bring an awareness of
some of the complex aspects of being a counsellor to a group. The focus of the
following codes and exercises is counselling. Other important tasks in supervision
include administration and management and social analysis.

1. SKILL PRACTICE SESSION OF SUPERVISING

Procedure

a. Participants are introduced to this
session as a key learning time for
developing the skills of supervising-
counselling. Participants will be in
groups of three's and each person will
have the opportunity to be a
supervisor, a person with a real
problem, and an observer.

b. Every one receives the handout called
'Choosing a Problem'. Give each
participant some time to choose an
actual problem.

c. Participants are asked to form groups
of threes and preferably groups
where they think a person could
honestly help them on their real problem. When they are in groups, have one
person first be the presenter of a problem. Another person is the supervisor,
and the third person is the observer (who is silent).

d. Now hand out the 'Framing of Questions in Supervision' paper. Have every
person read this and clarify any questions they might have.

e. Then hand out the 'Supervision Check List'. This will be used by the
Observer. Clarify any points necessary.

A — Supervisor
C — Observer
B — Presenter of Problem

*Most of the theory and handouts on supervision was adapted from CELT, Christian Education Leadership Training, South Africa.

142

Handout 1: **Choosing A Problem**

Select a problem with which you want help — a problem you would like to see more clearly.

1. It should be an important problem, but not so large that it cannot be helpfully discussed
2. It should be of real concern to you, something you care about.
3. It should be a problem in which you are involved.
4. It should be something you would like to see changed and something you believe could be changed.
5. It should be something in which you see yourself in relation to other people.
6. It may be something in which you are involved through a particular organisation, committee, or responsibility.
* It should **not** be a strictly personal or family problem.

Handout 2: **Framing of Questions in Supervision**

A guideline for supervisors

The use of questions in supervision often determines where your group facilitator goes in working through his or her task. Questions can communicate acceptance or rejection of the facilitator in your relationship. The framing of questions is a skill which is developed through experience.

Sometimes within the supervisory relationship you become confused and are not sure what problem to proceed with. Rather than to try to cover up your uncertainty and reduce trust which exists between you and the facilitator, it is more helpful to share your confusion with the facilitator. Ask him or her for help, work together in seeking to get moving again. In situations of uncertainty, we often destroy the progress we have made by our anxious response to 'give advice' or give ideas.

Major purposes of questions and comments

1. Indicate support and interest in the other.
2. Focus on important information.
3. Encourage deeper examination. Why does something happen?
4. Open up new areas.
5. Clarify group leaders' or facilitator's position and relationship to participants.
6. Help facilitator to evaluate without defensiveness.
7. Enable the facilitator to make decisions and help him or her to see what will happen if they stick to a decision (what are the consequences).
8. Provide resources when needed.

Handout 3: **Supervision check list**
(For observer)

DO's
1. Did the supervisor use **two-way communication**? How?
2. Was this a **joint exploration**? (a shared search together?)
3. Was the supervisor a good **listener**? When not?
4. Did the supervisor try to **reduce threat**? Defensiveness?
5. Was (s)he **non-judgmental**?
6. Were questions **helpful** and clarifying?

DON'T's
1. Did the supervisor **tell** or give advice? Was advice ever asked for?
2. Did (s)he **show-off** her or his own knowledge?
3. Did (s)he argue for his or her own views?
4. Was (s)he **honest**?
5. Did the supervisor **interrupt** or stop the person from talking when it did not seem appropriate?

Time: 10 minutes to introduce the practice session.
Go over 'Choosing a Problem' handout.
10 minutes to form groups of 3's and go over
'Framing Questions' and 'Supervision Check List' handouts.
20 minutes. Round 1. One person presents her or his problem. Another person is the supervisor and the third person is the observer.
10 minutes. The observer gives feedback to the supervisor. All 3 people discuss the **process** of the help given, they should not continue to discuss the content of the problem.
Begin Round 2. A different person is the presenter of a problem, a different person is supervisor and a different person is observer. Use the same procedure as described above.
Begin Round 3. Use the same process rotating people to different roles.
This exercise will take a minimum of 2 hours.

Final Discussion.   In the whole group discuss:

1.   What have we learnt about being a supervisor?

Materials

Newsprint, markers, tape.
3 Handouts as indicated above on separate paper, enough for each participant to have one copy of each.
A large room so groups can hear each other well.

144

2. CREATIVE USE OF OPPOSITION*

In life we often find two kinds of responses to our work or our ideas. One kind is supportive; the other is opposition, resistance, differences or correction. If we offer an idea for action to a parish council, or we make a statement to our group, the response may be agreeing, supporting, or building on what we have said. However, it may be opposing, pointing out faults or errors, or resisting what we have said.

> Supportive: 'I think what you said is a good idea.'
> 'I think you are right and I would like to add. . . .'
> Opposing: 'I cannot agree with that.'
> 'Can't you see how wrong you are?'

Both the supportive and opposing are real forces in life. They can be used or not be used. It is usually very easy to use the supporting responses. However, many times we do not use the real value of forces which are in opposition.

Ideas are always expressed by **persons**, and therefore when one person's idea is opposing another person's idea, the **person** is also opposing the other **person**. How we then see the other person's idea is not always clear and hostility is usually present because ideas which seem to be very sound and logical, also have a personal **feeling behind them.** For example, if someone opposed **my** idea, I can receive this opposition as if it is directed to me personally. The result is that we often mistake a strong challenger as an enemy when that person is perhaps our sister or brother.

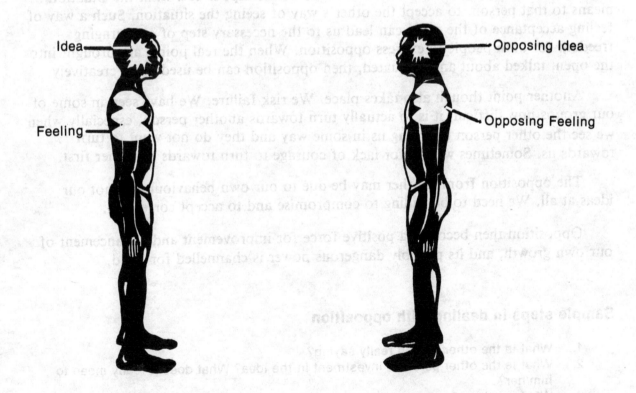

* Adapted from an article by Tom Conway, *Basic Reader in Human Relations Training*, Part 1, pp. 116-118.

We can approach opposition in three ways:

1. We can resist it. We can **fight** like a lion. This is the most usual way. Hostility is met with hostility, anger is met with anger.
2. We can **avoid** or deny the opposition like **an ostrich.** We can just pay no attention to what they say. Another way to avoid opposition is to submit to the opposing idea, just give in, like a rabbit.
3. The third approach to opposition is to use it. **We** very much **need** what our opposition has to offer. We all need help to come to better ideas. Opposition can be seen as offering correction.

However, this approach involves us more. It means we need to turn towards that person, neither avoiding nor resisting that person, but truly **turning towards that person.** It means we must see the other person as a human being, and because they are human, they have dignity and worth.

> The other person has feelings,
> has the possibility of changing,
> has not got the whole truth,
> **just like us.**

Therefore, if we can listen to and learn from the other person's opposing ideas and actions, we can grow.

In this turning towards the other person, we attempt to feel what the situation means to that person, to accept the other's way of seeing the situation. Such a way of feeling acceptance of the other can lead us to the necessary step of encouraging freedom for both people to express opposition. When the real points are brought into the open, talked about and evaluated, then opposition can be used more creatively.

Another point though also takes place. We risk failure. We have seen in some of our groups how difficult it is to actually turn towards another person, especially when we see the other person opposing us in some way and they do not want to turn towards us. Sometimes we fail for lack of courage to turn towards the other first.

The opposition from another may be due to our own behaviour and not our ideas at all. We need to be willing to compromise and to accept correction.

Opposition then becomes a positive force for improvement and advancement of our own growth, and its possibly dangerous power is channelled for good.

Sample steps in dealing with opposition

1. What is the other person **really** saying?
2. What is the other person's investment in the idea? What does it really mean to him/her?
3. What are the other person's feelings?
   What are the other person's feelings about me?
   What are my feelings about the other person?
4. What are the strengths of the other person's ideas or position?
5. How might they be applied to my ideas?

Ways of dealing with opposition

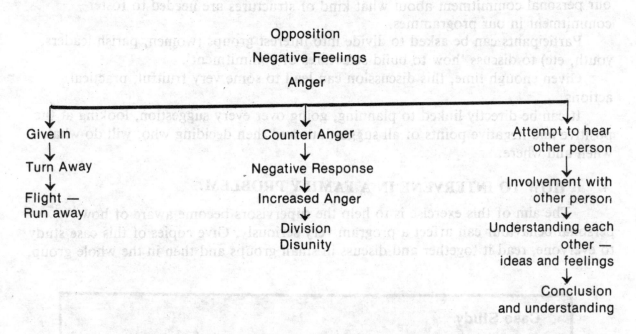

The above input can be given in summary form either before or after this exercise. In order to understand conflict and how we react to it, it is best to look at ourselves first. There is no way we can help others who are in conflict if we have very little self-knowledge about how we ourselves deal with conflict.

Discussion Questions: Ask people to find a partner they can easily talk with. In partners, for about half an hour, discuss the following questions. As facilitator you can decide whether some or none of this should be shared in the whole group.

1. Think of a strong experience of when someone has opposed you.
2. What were you fighting for? What was the other fighting for?
3. What animal were you most like then?
4. Now at a distance, can you get 'into their shoes' and appreciate why they opposed you?

3. REFLECTION ON COMMITMENT

No baby is born with commitment. No commitment is static. It is a living thing like a plant, that grows and develops, or declines and dies, as a result of specific conditions and experiences.

Think of your own commitment. (Everyone has a paper and pen — give them time quietly to think.) You can think of it as a plant, or some symbol or a diagram. Now draw your symbol, reflecting on the life of your commitment — its history. Ask yourself the following questions:

— when and how was the seed planted?
— what fostered its early growth?
— did you have an experience that threatened the continuation
— of its life?
— what has strengthened the plant — the commitment?
— what conditions does it long for that would strengthen it now?

Time: 15 minutes of silent individual reflection-drawing.

30 minutes to share in groups of six. If you have less time — share in partners.

147

After this exercise — and a break, it is possible to build on our insights into our personal commitment about what kind of structures are needed to foster commitment in our programmes.

Participants can be asked to divide into interest groups (women, parish leaders, youth, etc) to discuss 'how to build structures of commitment'.

Given enough time, this discussion can lead to some very fruitful, practical actions.

It can be directly linked to planning, going over every suggestion, looking at the positive and negative points of all suggestions and then deciding who, will do what, when and where.

4. HOW TO INTERVENE IN A FAMILY PROBLEM?

The aim of this exercise is to help the supervisors become aware of how personal behaviour can affect a program very seriously. Give copies of this case study to everyone, read it together and discuss in small groups and then in the whole group.

Case Study

At a parish development workshop a group of people from the sub-station of Kilimeni decided that they wanted a literacy class. They were told to find someone who lived nearby who would be willing to teach the class and to send him to the next diocesan training programme for literacy teachers. James Ndege, a young man of 24 who had completed Form II and was now working on his father's farm, was asked to do this job. He agreed enthusiastically, did very well in the training and soon had a good class of 20 people meeting three times a week.

One of the participants was a lively young married woman called Josephine Namanga. She joined actively in the class discussions, and often stayed after class to continue discussing some points with James, the literacy teacher, and two other men in the class. Because of paying more and more attention to Josephine in class the teacher gradually ignored the other participants. Because of this, Josephine was often getting home late. One day he approached Josephine and tried to persuade her to come home with him, but she refused saying she was only interested in learning to read and write, and to improve the life of her family. James became very persistent but Josephine still refused.

However, her husband Thomas had become angry and suspicious because Josephine was always coming home late. One day he beat her and the next evening when both he and James were drinking in the bar, he accused James of being in love with her. James said he had done nothing but that Josephine was constantly trying to approach him.

Soon this story was all round the village. Many of the other participants in the literacy class were disgusted and stopped coming to class.

The supervisor had visited this class twice and it was going well at that time.

Questions

Imagine that you are the supervisor of James Ndege, the Literacy teacher:

1. How could you deal with this situation now?
2. What different problems can be identified?

3. Who would you think it necessary to talk to, and
    What would your approach be with each person?
4. What changes, if any, would be necessary in the programme?

5. SKILLS OF A GOOD SUPERVISOR

The supervisor needs a genuine concern and interest in the success of each group leader as well as the success of the programme as a whole.

1. **Listening:** The first skill needed is the ability to listen carefully, picking out both positive aspects, and problems, difficulties, tensions in the situation.

2. **Observation:** Going closely with listening is observation — the ability to pick up information about the situation — the feelings from non-verbal cues.

3. **Empathy:** The supervisor needs to be able to identify with the problems as seen through the eyes of the group leader (e.g. How does the group leader feel if the codes, exercise books, etc. have not arrived on time?).

4. **Helpful questioning:** Sympathetic questioning that enables the group leader
    — to identify the weaknesses in his/her own leadership so far,
    — to understand the causes of problems,
    — to think through the consequences of certain types of actions, etc.
    is much more helpful than the statement of opinions and judgements by the supervisor.

5. **Encouragement:** The supervisor needs to build the confidence of the group leaders by affirming the positive aspects of the work done showing appreciation for the time and commitment given, and by helping them to recognise the negative aspects for themselves, thinking out alternative ways of doing things.

6. **Summarizing:** The supervisor needs to be able to summarize the information that (s)he has picked up from the situation in many different ways, picking out the main problems, different possibilities, etc.

7. **Mutual learning:** Supervisors who think they know all the answers are not helpful. A willingness to learn from the group leader and the group is important in creating a good spirit and learning climate.

8. **Flexibility:** Every programme needs to be adapted to the special circumstances and needs of the people and place of the group. The supervisor needs to be flexible in order to encourage flexibility, creativity and a spirit of experimentation in each group leader. Creative group leaders are much more effective than those who merely copy what their trainers have done. The supervisor needs to encourage experiments but also an evaluation of each experiment by the creative group leader.

9. **Timing:** The supervisor needs a sense of timing, when to encourage, when to challenge, when to ask a question, give a suggestion, give support.

10. **Planning:** The role of the supervisor in the specific programme will demand a certain amount of planning. The supervisor needs to be aware of how he uses time; how to distribute materials **on time**; how to meet reasonable requests from group leaders realistically; and how to be a good example in planning which will also reflect a model for the group leaders. Good planning by the supervisor can mean better planning by the group leaders.

6. PROBLEMS OF A SUPERVISOR

Certain tensions are often present between a supervisor and the group leaders who are being supervised. These can be reduced if the supervisor is aware that these difficulties are to be expected, and learns how to deal with them constructively.

Reactions to Authority: Supervisors have authority both because of their position and appointment by the organisers of the programme; and because of their knowledge and experience as group leaders (literacy teachers, etc.). If they throw this authority around they may either overwhelm new group leaders and reduce their confidence, or in a different type of personality, cause counter-dependence or resistance to every suggestion they make.

Insecurity of the group leader: We all feel insecure when we start a new job and it is natural that new group leaders should fear criticism and having their mistakes pointed out. They are still trying to establish a good relationship with their group and so they are particularly sensitive to criticism in front of the group.

Dependency: Some group leaders become dependent on their supervisors and want them to make all the important decisions. The supervisor needs to help the group leaders to stand on their own feet by helping them to think through problems and make responsible decisions themselves.

Resistance to an outsider: The supervisor must realize that in certain ways they are 'outsiders' whereas the group leader has regular contact with the participants and feels like an 'insider'. It is therefore extremely important to take time to listen carefully to the problems of the group leader; not offering suggestions and solutions too quickly showing that you do not understand the problem fully.

Trying to impress: Some supervisors are more concerned to show off their own expertise, and to get quick results in the programme, than to develop the skill, confidence and commitment of the new leader.

Conflicting loyalties of the Supervisor: Supervisors are often torn between their concern for the group participants and their loyalty to the group organising the programme, and their concern for the growth of the group leader in skill and confidence. The growth of the group leader is of primary importance because in that way the participants and the whole programme will automatically benefit.

7. THE SUPERVISOR'S ROLE — ENABLING OTHERS TO GROW

The role of the supervisor is not primarily to see that the work gets done well, but to see that those doing the work are constantly growing in commitment and skill, so that they have motivation from within themselves, not merely pressure from someone outside, to do the work as well as possible. This internal motivation arises both from

- a strong identification with the goals of the work, (This can be helped by shared goal setting and planning.)
- a clear understanding of their own role,
- confidence in their own ability to carry out this role (good methods),
- understanding of the roles of others.
- relationships which enable them to discuss success and failures in an open, supportive atmosphere.

What **conditions** enable us to **grow**?

We need a combination of challenge and support. First of all we need a basic atmosphere of Acceptance and Appreciation. An important aspect of this is that somebody is willing to take time with us, listening to our concerns, rejoicing in our successes and entering into our own experience of failure without judging us harshly. But besides this we also need challenge. This is first of all a challenge to get more deeply involved in the overall goals of the programme. Besides this we need a deeper awareness of our own potential. Feedback is designed to build a person's confidence and skill and commitment. Negative feedback is sometimes necessary, but it is only helpful if there is first a sense of appreciation, and confidence that one can do a good job.

Some growth is smooth and regular, as a small fish grows into a big fish. But there are other times when growth involves painful and alarming change, as when a tadpole grows into a frog.

This is the type of change that is happening when someone has to change from a teacher into a group facilitator. It is not easy and the person needs a lot of help to understand what is going on. But then suddenly the little creature finds instead of swimming peacefully round in nice familiar water, she is becoming a funny shape, growing new arms and legs. At first they seem ugly and awkward, but soon she finds she can actually jump. The whole world opens up with new possibilities. It is far more exciting to be a frog than a tadpole, but one needs encouragement during the time of change.

> Africa must refuse to be humiliated, exploited and pushed about.
> And with the same determination we must refuse to humiliate, exploit or push others around. We must act, not just say words.
>
> Julius Nyerere
> **Freedom and Development**, p. 371.

Chapter 12

Planning Workshops

This chapter includes:

There are seven stages necessary in carrying out a workshop (or a planned learning experience). The event may be a one hour session, a series of evenings, a one-day program, or a week-long workshop. No matter how short or long, all stages are important.

1. Pre-planning.
2. Gathering information (about the needs and concerns of participants).
3. Analysing information.
4. Deciding on the aim of the event.
5. Designing the event.
6. Carrying out the event.
7. Evaluating the event.

Chapter 12

Planning Workshops

1. GUIDELINES FOR PRE-PLANNING A LEARNING EVENT

a. **Broad aim:** Why is the workshop needed? What is the purpose? What is the long-term aim?

b. **Participants:** What kind of participants need to be invited? (men, women, youth, educational background, common interests, etc.) Is it open to all or just by invitation? How many people should we have? Will we accept individuals or only teams? Do we want definite replies or can the event be open to whoever comes?

c. **Data collection:** How do we plan to get the needs and interests of the participants? (See Chapter 2 on survey.)

d. **Staff team:** Who do we need? How many staff? Who is co-ordinator? What is his/her role? Do we need any special resource people? Will they expect fees? Staff planning time. How much is needed? When? Where? Expectations of staff and commitment of staff to the program and their time.

e. **Place:** Where will we hold it? Is it easy for the participants to reach? (but not so close to home they will be distracted by everyday responsibilities.) Is the working space suitable? Is the accommodation suitable for overnight courses? Is it available? Is the booking definite?

f. **Time:** How long should it be? One session? Several sessions? Is it a convenient time for participants and staff (school holidays, planting time, etc.) Can they be away that long? (from babies, work responsibilities, etc.).

g. **Publicity:** How will you invite people? Leaflets? Posters? Letters? Word of mouth?

h. **Housekeeping details:** Cost. What food, if any, do you need? Suitable clothes? Map to the place, etc.

2.   Gathering Information

We need the following information about participants.
—   What are the main concerns and needs, their hopes and worries?
—   What problems do they have in common?
—   Why are they coming to this workshop?
—   What are their attitudes to these problems?
—   What skills do they want to practise?

3.   Analysing Information

Once we have found what the participants are interested in we need to find out at what level they want to deal with each subject.
Do they want to develop their own awareness,
—   to obtain information,
—   to analyse the root causes of a problem,
—   to make plans for action,
—   to deal with the feelings involved,
—   to practise particular skills they need?

Your aim and your design should be based on both their concern and the level at which the participants are wishing to deal with the concern. The satisfaction of the participants will depend on how you can meet both these needs.

4.   Deciding on the Aim of the Event

Usually our long term aims are very broad but we cannot accomplish everything in one workshop. We need to decide on a definite limited aim which can be accomplished in the **time** available, and with the **staff** and **money** available.

It is important that the Staff all agree on this **aim** or they may pull in different directions during the actual workshop. Therefore it is advisable that they prepare together a short clear written statement of the aim. It should show the level you plan to deal with the subject.

Check your aim

1.   Is it relevant to the participants?
       (not what we think they need, but what *they* think they need).
2.   Is it based on their life, experience, concerns?
3.   Does it show either
       (a)   a process of discovery leading to deeper understanding,
       or (b)   a process of planning,
       or (c)   practice of a skill they want.
4.   Is it clear?
5.   Is it possible in the *time* available?
6.   Is the problem area too large? Do we need to limit it further?
7.   Can we as *staff* carry it out or do we need extra resource people?

5.   DESIGNING THE EVENT

Basic Principles:

The design needs to make sure that the 4 needs of participants mentioned by Gibb are all provided for so that a spirit of community and trust may grow in the group. These 4 needs are:

— Acceptance,
— Sharing Information,
— Setting Goals, and
— Organising for Action. (See Chapter 5 for details.)

The basic 'learning process' should be taken into account:

— DO,
— LOOK,
— THINK (and get more information if necessary)
— CHANGE.

The design needs to provide for
— Reflection on Experience and
— Planning for Future Action.

Every workshop should include:

a.   An opportunity for participants to **get to know each other** and feel at ease in the group. (E.g. introductions at the beginning and trust building exercises later.)

   In short meetings these introductions have to be rather quick but if all the participants do not know one another, they are essential. Otherwise the group will not recognise or make use of the possible contributions of all members. In longer workshops introductions should be given enough time, as this is the first step in building trust and community.

b.   An opportunity to **share their concerns**, hopes and worries, and their expectations of this particular workshop. Even if the staff have gathered information beforehand, the participants need to share concerns with each other. The planning group will base the programme on these concerns.

   In short events this has usually been done beforehand. In longer workshops the programme should constantly be adjusted to meet the concerns as they become clear.

c.   A common experience (or a reminder of a common experience).

   A workshop may contain a number of these within the overall design.

   As the experience of participants 'at home' may often be very varied and may take a long time to explain, it is often helpful to provide a common experience, which each one can link to their own previous experience. This is like the match that starts the fire of discussion. One must involve their hearts as well as their heads.

This experience can be:

- looking at a poster
  play
  film
- listening to a story
- reading a case study
- singing a song
- creating a collage
  symbol
  display
  drawing
  dance
- choosing a photograph
- taking part in a
  - role play
  - simulation (Star Power, Rural Money Game)
  - exercise (listening Pairs,
    Co-operative Squares,
    Build with What you've Got,
    Multiple Role
    Fishbowl.
- going on a field trip.

These experiences should be directly related to the common concerns expressed.

d. An opportunity for participants to **look** carefully at what happened, and to describe it as objectively as possible.

e. An opportunity to **link** this **with** their **own experience**, and share their insight into the problems related to this concern. This should not be hurried as listening attentively to one another is an important means of raising awareness.

f. An opportunity to **analyse the causes of the problems** that have been raised. Careful questions from the leaders should help the participants move from symptoms to the root causes.

g. **Plan** what can be done in the future. Such tools as:
  - Force Field Analysis
  - 3 C's
  - 7 Steps
    can be very helpful here. Sometimes this involves learning
    or practising new skills, e.g.
    - chairing a discussion,
    - reaching a decision,
    - dealing with an angry person,
    - trying out new behaviour.

Role play and reverse role play can be used for some of these.

6. ADMINISTERING THE PLAN

a.   **Roles of participants and staff during the event:** Remember: It is
the **participants** who should have an **experience**,
the **participants** who look at **what happened**,
the **participants** who **analyse** the experience,
the **participants** who **plan action**.

The role of the staff is to help the participants do this. Staff direct,
observe, and raise questions when necessary, but if they take over the
discussions, they **defeat** the purpose of experience-centred learning. They
become 'teachers-telling-the-answers' rather than facilitators enabling the
participants to discover for themselves.

b.   **Some general principles for administering a plan:**

— **Know your plan:** Be clear on all the details.

— **Check details beforehand:** The lack of a piece of masking tape, or chalk
at the crucial time, can ruin a programme.

— **Trust your plan:** You have worked hard on it. It is the best thing
available to start with.

— **But do not worship your plan:** It may become clear as time progresses,
that it will not work. Be willing to make adjustments,
or even change it completely if necessary. It did not
come from heaven.

— **Trust the group:** They want the time to be fruitful and are concerned
for one another. They too have resources.

— **Trust yourselves:** If necessary find an opportunity for staff consultation
together. (e.g. when participants are discussing in
small groups.)

— **Do not waste an experience:** Even if the plan seems to fall flat,
remember that 'mistakes' can be the most valuable
learning experiences.

— **Be human:**   You do not need to pretend to know everything,
and never make mistakes.

Evaluating the event

An opportunity to evaluate the event and for participants to express their
feelings about it is usually a very helpful part of a workshop. Especially if the event
has been a little frustrating, this can become the liveliest part of the whole event, and,
if the leaders are not defensive, one of the parts where everyone gets the most
valuable learning.

This should be done for separate events within a workshop and for the workshop
as a whole. Several exercises are suggested for this in Chapter 8.

An Exercise on How to Organise a Workshop

In Chapter 7 you will find an exercise and a practice model of how to organise
a workshop. This can especially be helpful to plan and learn the skills of
management.

Possible Designs for different kinds of workshops

Just as every session within a workshop should have an objective, each workshop should have a clear focus. The focus must take into account:

1. What are the needs of this group?
2. What are the problems facing this group?
3. What would this group like to accomplish by the end of the workshop?

The planning team for a workshop needs to meet before the workshop with people from that area, for example, a diocesan team needs to meet with some of the youth before a workshop for that particular group. At this preliminary meeting, the focus of the workshop needs to be decided.

The following designs are listed only as guidelines of what to include in a workshop and to show how different kinds of workshops can be designed. Of course, there are many other possibilities and a variety of elements for different needs may have to be included in any workshop. For example, in a development workshop a common problem may be communication between two groups (staff and workers or priests and laity) and therefore an exercise to clarify the problems between these two groups may be needed in that workshop.

1. **Development Workshop** (see Chapters 3 and 7)

   a. Introductions
   b. Listening Exercise
   c. What is Development?
   d. Maslow's Ladder of Human Needs
   e. Hopes and Worries about development
   f. Expectations for this workshop
   g. Approaches to community needs
   h. Animators choose or prepare codes on the main themes raised by the group
      (see chapter 3 for ideas)
   i. Interest groups formed to go deeper into problems raised, using force field analysis
      or 7-Steps of planning (see chapter 7 for details)
   j. Area groups for planning follow-up
   k. Final evaluation of workshop
      (mid-point evaluation somewhere between h and i)

2. **Problem posing Method Workshop** (See Chapters 2, 3 and 4)

   For those responsible for preparing and running adult education programs (not animators who will need prepared materials and sets of codes).

   a. Introductions
   b. Listening exercise
   c. Aim of the problem posing method in development
   d. How adults learn and other exercises in chapter 4
   e. CDO Play, approaches to development
   f. Theory behind method
   g. Area groups to plan use of method back home
   h. Final evaluation of workshop
      (mid-point evaluation can happen after 'f')

3. **Problem posing Method Workshop** (for literacy animators) See Chapters 2, 3, and 4)

   a. Introductions
   b. Listening exercises
   c. Find out their ideas of main problems in the area
   d. Demonstrate use of a code on one of the themes they have raised
   e. Theory of awareness and response
   f. Stages of method: survey, themes, etc.
   g. 3 ways codes have been used
   h. What does a good animator do when using a code?
   i. Johari's window
   j. Practice for each person in leading discussion on a code in small groups.
      i. preparation of questions on code chosen,
      ii. each person leads one discussion,
      iii. evaluation of code and leadership after each discussion
   k. Summary of differences between problem posing method and traditional teaching methods
   l. Literacy practice sessions
   m. Evaluation of workshop

4. **Leadership or Group Methods Workshop** (See Chapters 5 and 6)

   a. Introductions
   b. Listening exercise
   c. Types of leadership exercise
   d. What does a good leader do in a group?
   e. Co-operative squares, jigsaw cow, or 'Build What-you've Got'
   f. Johari's window
   g. Feedback exercises
   h. Mid-point evaluation
   i. Fishbowl — POPO and task and maintenance
   j. Other leadership exercises
   k. Decision-making exercises and theory
   l. Planning exercises for follow-up
   m. Final evaluation of workshop

5. **Communications Workshops** (See Chapters 5, 6 and 10)

   a. Introductions
   b. Trust building exercise if they know each other otherwise use it later
   c. Listening exercises
   d. Johari's window.
   e. Appreciate/find difficult/request
   f. Other exercises in chapter 6 and 10
   g. Co-operative squares or build with what you've got.
   h. Plan follow-up
   i. Final evaluation of workshop

6. **Planning Workshop** (See Chapters 3 and 7)

   a. Introductions
   b. Listening exercise
   c. Problems of development they are experiencing
   d. Expectations for this workshop
   e. Reflections on development
   f. Animators choose or prepare several codes on main themes to deepen awareness and analyse causes (see Chapters 3 and 9)
   g. Mid-point evaluation
   h. Exercises/theory on decision-making/approaches to basic needs
   i. Exercise on planning (see Chapter 7)
   j. Final evaluation of workshop

7.   **Supervisors Workshop** (See Chapter 11)

   a.   Introductions
   b.   Listening exercise
   c.   Problem survey
   d.   Clarification on role of a supervisor
   e.   Listening techniques
   f.   Skill practice session of supervising
   h.   How to intervene in a family problem
   i.   Reflection on commitment
   j.   Discussion on tasks of supervisors
   k.   Plan implementation and changes
   l.   Evaluation of workshop

8.   **Administration and Management Workshop** (See Chapters 10 and 11)

   a.   Introductions
   b.   Listening exercise
   c.   Problem survey or expectations
   d.   Corruption code
   e.   Personal and public funds
   f.   Commitment cycle
   g.   Theory X and Y
   h.   Simple accounts skill practice
   i.   Report writing
   j.   The planning kit
   k.   An exercise on team management
   l.   A challenge to organise
   m.   Plan implementation and changes in your organisation
   n.   Final evaluation of workshop

9.   **Organisational Development Workshop** (See Chapter 10)

   a.   Introductions
   b.   Listening exercise
   c.   The parabola
   d.   An exercise to clarify vision
   e.   Vision statement
   f.   Codes on assumptions
   g.   Setting goals
   h.   Commitment cycle
   i.   Delegation skills
   j.   Clarifying roles
   k.   Planning implementation and changes
   l.   Final evaluation of workshop

10. **Participatory Evaluation Workshop** (See Chapter 8)

   a. Introductions
   b. Listening exercise
   c. What is evaluation?
   d. Evaluation exercise
   e. Problems of evaluation
   f. Why do we evaluate?
   g. When do we evaluate?
   h. Ethics of evaluation
   i. Planning questions and indicators of evaluation
   j. Methods of evaluation
   k. Planning a program for evaluation
   l. Final evaluation of workshop

11. **Social Analysis Workshop** (See Chapter 9)

   Preparation. Participants do research on their own situation using the economic (or other) analysis questionnaires found in chapter 9.

   a. Introductions
      Class Origin/Class Option
   b. Listening Exercise.
      Listening pairs found in chapter 5.
   c. Shape of the World exercise
   d. The Door exercise
   e. Three Storey Building input
   f. Input on Visual Presentation of research collected
   g. Preparation of charts and diagrams of local and wider level.
   h. Sharing of material using charts as codes.
   i. Input on the economic (or other) situation using the relevant models from chapter 9 (e.g. centre/ periphery).
   j. Star Power and discussion using further models from chapter 9.
   k. Group work making codes and discussion outlines to deal with local economic situation.
   l. Critique of codes.
   m. Evaluation of workshop.

Outline of the DELTA program for training trainers

We found that the most effective way to train those who would later train others to use this method, was an in-service program spread over about a year. It involved four one-week workshops, one every two or three months and in between workshops, the application of the methods learnt, by the teams in their own situation. Only teams who could work together were accepted for the program. Each workshop ended with planning real programs to be carried out within the next couple of months, and the next workshop began with an evaluation of this application.

Phase 1 focused on the problem-posing method, with skill practice in developing and using codes and question outlines. It also included planning how teams could start using the method in their own situations.

Phase 2 usually dealt with trust building and went more deeply into shared leadership, self and mutual criticism.

Phase 3 dealt with building a movement, the need for different forms of management, structures, authority, and included work on the vision of a new society.

Phase 4 linked the issues that had been emerging in their concrete work with an analysis of the wider society at a deeper level.

A model we found helpful was:

> Begin with the issues of the local community and ways of getting people actively involved;
> move to individual leadership skills, self-knowledge, and team work.
> Look at institutions and organisations, and
> go back to a deeper analysis of society and long-term planning.

Each workshop needs to be a whole in itself but each one builds on the other. Participants were asked to commit themselves to all phases so that trust and solidarity could grow.

Women's Training

In most institutions, men are usually the ones chosen or appointed to attend courses. This has put women in the position of never being able to 'catch up'. The DELTA training program insisted on balanced teams, but this often did not work out in practice.

In order to build up the women's skills and experience a separate women's training program was developed which was shorter and focused on the immediate problems facing women.

The same general approach was used, starting with the issues of the local community, moving to leadership skills, and then to planning more practical projects.

Theology and development workshop

The following is a combination of a workshop, seminar and retreat. **Training for Transformation** is solidly based on the theology of Vatican II. When working with Christian groups, it is important to organise this type of workshop to help those involved in the program to understand the theological basis of what they are doing.

All 'Reflections' in this section are from short lectures by **Fr. Brian Hearne** C.S.Sp. who currently teaches at GABA Pastoral Institute, Eldoret, Kenya and who helped in a workshop intitled, 'Theology and Development', in 1979.

> 'Orthopraxis, that is the true living of the Christian faith, is even more important than Orthodoxy, the intellectual acceptance of the true teaching of the church.'

A theology and development workshop should try to build a community of trust in which the participants:

a. become aware of Christ's presence among them,
b. reflect on — their own personal experience, and
— what they see happening in the world,
c. link this to the theological teaching of the church,
d. pray, individually and communally, about the implications of all the above in their lives,
e. celebrate both the promise and the experience of salvation,
f. plan how to make all the new insights, about the role of the church as charismatic community committed to development and liberation, into a living reality in their own situation.

> 'The truth is only the truth, when it is lived.'

The following is one example of how theological reflection can be built into a workshop with people actively involved in development. Of course the topics would vary according to the priorities of the group.

Each section contains:

a. an exercise, code or questions to help the participants play an active role in the theological reflection, and
b. a summary of input given by Fr. Brian Hearne, C.S.Sp. from GABA Pastoral Institute, Kenya.

1. BUILDING A TEMPORARY COMMUNITY

The church is a charismatic community drawn together by the Holy Spirit and committed to transformation.

Introductions and expectations

Procedure

In order to make the workshop into a real experience of community it is important to start building a spirit of trust through meaningful introductions, giving everybody an opportunity to share something of themselves and to start getting to know all the others in a human and personal way.

This community building continues in sharing the expectations of the participants to make sure that their real concerns are taken into account during the workshop. It can also be helpful to do a listening exercise at this stage.

Reflection

In this workshop the importance of small Christian communities will be discussed. Usually we think of geographical living communities, but the spirit of community needs to exist in many forms. Very often small temporary communities have been extremely significant in providing Christians with a new awareness and an experience of the church, as a charismatic community. In such temporary communities, many Christians have found the motivation for a new level of commitment to 'the Kingdom' and to the process of liberation and transformation.

Jesus was not just a preacher talking about the Kingdom. He was actively involved in the practical work of establishing this Kingdom of Justice, Peace and Love.

"Christ proclaims salvation, this great gift of God, which is Liberation from everything that oppresses human beings, but which is above all, liberation from sin and the evil one. . . . All of this is begun during the life of Christ, and definitely accomplished by His death and resurrection. But it must be patiently carried on during the course of history, in order to be realised fully on the day of the coming of Christ."

— Evangelii Nuntiandi, No. 9

The church is a charismatic community of believers drawn together by the Holy Spirit to continue Christ's work of liberation and to give witness to the existence of the Kingdom among us.

"Only the Kingdom is absolute, and it makes everything else relative."

— Evangelii Nuntiandi, No. 15.

There is no opposition between the task of liberation at any level, and the proclamation of the coming Kingdom. In fact the most effective way of proclaiming God's Kingdom may be the work of liberation in society.

Our belief in the Incarnation implies the sacredness of the whole material world. The world is the place where Salvation is worked out . . . it is the place that God loves . . . it cannot be evil. Resurrection includes the taking up to God of the whole material universe. The whole of the universe has been sanctified and each person has been sealed again with the mark of a personality made in the image of God.

To speak in terms of evangelising, as if it meant only the proclamation of the Good News, is in fact to ignore the reality of Christian faith. As Christians, we are called to take an active role in making Christ's promise a reality for everybody: 'I have come that you may have life, and have it to the full.'

As St Irenaeus said, 'The Glory of God is man fully alive, and the life of man is the vision of God.' ('Man' here means both the individual woman or man, and the whole human race.)

Liberation for the Christian is thus freedom from all forms of oppression: social, economic, political, ideological, and spiritual and more than this. It is transcendence, a new life of love in a transformed world.

2. THE CHURCH IN DIALOGUE WITH THE WORLD

To fulfill her mission, the church must live in dialogue with the world, listening and learning from the world, and responding to the Signs of the Times.

Procedure: Shape of the World Exercise

This is an excellent exercise to help your group reflect on the 'Signs of the Times'. The exercise can also be done on a district or national level and the instructions are found on page 15, Book 3. It is helpful to have a resource person present to give some factual background on certain issues where there is likely to be a wide range of perception.

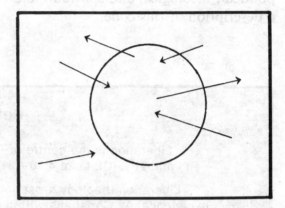

Reflection

From very early times the church taught that God reveals himself to us in three books:

— the Bible,
— the Human Spirit (the whole human experience)
— the World (creation)

In Vatican II the church again stressed very strongly the need for the church to get out of the defensive closed mentality of the Post-Reformation church, where it seemed as if 'one had to get out of the world, to get into the kingdom'. The Bishops wrote, 'The church looks at the world, with hope and with affection'.

The church recognised her role to be in meaningful dialogue with the world. This involved not only proclaiming the message but also hearing, listening, and learning. And as she listened, the cries of oppression, exploitation and suffering became very distinct. This meant that in trying to put into practice the theology of Vatican II, the church was led inevitably to liberation theology. It was because the Latin American church was listening to the needs of the world, that liberation theology emerged at the meeting of the Bishops at Medellin in 1968.

Liberation is the centre of Christ's message and of his own mission and ministry. (Cf. Luke 4:16 – 21)

3.   **TOTAL LIBERATION.** From what? Towards what?

Procedure: The Liberator Code.

The Liberator Code is a one minute mime and easy to prepare. It opens up an important discussion on the ways in which we are enslaved (economic, social, political, ideological and spiritual) and on true and false liberation. See chapter 3 for a description of this code.

Reflection

Liberation is the centre of Christ's message and of his own mission and ministry. (Cf. Luke 4:16 – 21)

Liberation theology arose initially from reflection on the human experience. As Christians with a renewed interest in the Gospels tried more seriously to respond to the needs of the poor, it became clear that a great deal of their suffering was not inevitable, was certainly not the will of God, but was caused by the greed and heartlessness of other people. They recognised man-made exploitation and oppression on a vast scale. As they searched for God's response to this situation of human suffering, they turned to three main sources of influence in the Bible:

— the story of the Exodus,
— the Prophets (especially Amos, Hosea, Isaiah, Jeremiah and Deuteronomy)
— the life of Jesus

The Exodus is the central event of the Old Testament, showing most decisively God's loving concern for the oppressed. Exodus reveals God as the God of the oppressed, actively intervening in history to set his people free.

The Prophets strongly denounce oppression and exploitation of the weak and defenceless, and call upon the people to be just, concerned for the poor and afflicted, as Yahweh Himself is concerned.

All the actions, the parables and the teaching of Jesus show his deep concern for the poor, and his challenge to the rich and powerful. He is a revolutionary in the deepest sense, turning upside down the values of this world, and it is very clear that in the Kingdom he is establishing, the poor and those who hunger and thirst for justice have a special place.

---

4.   **CO-CREATION**

The Exercise: Life line

Life line is a trust building exercise which can deepen relationships in the workshop community through personal sharing. Participants can be asked to draw their life line focussing especially on those events and experiences in which they were most conscious of God's intervention in their own lives and the people who helped them to become the person they now are. See chapter 5 for details about this exercise.

Reflection

As we draw our own life lines, and listen to the story of each others lives, we become very conscious of the absolute uniqueness of each person's story. But then gradually, linking up all these stories, we find the story of God.

Life is the creative interaction between two stories; the unique personal history of each of us and the story of God. He is present in all of human history, and in all the things that happen to us. This interaction takes place in our lives to the extent that we are open to the story of others. In knowing more about one another we know more about God. The tension in every religion of how the individual story meets the story of God, is resolved for us in the story of Jesus Christ. In him we find the definition of what it means to he human. In the life of Jesus, God's life becomes the human story.

As we reflect on our lives we can often see how God has acted in our lives through other people. He has called them to co-create us. This is one of the deepest ways in which we can understand what it means that we are made in the image of God. God is the great creator, but He has called us not only to share in the creation of the world, but even to share in the co-creation of one another.

One cannot say that all people are equally made in the image of God. Of course we cannot judge, but we know that it is to the extent that we become co-creators with him of our fellow human beings, enabling them to become more and more fully human, as Jesus was most fully human, that we grow more and more into the image of God. This is our human and divine vocation, to be co-creators of one another.

A life line is a story of a pilgrim, moving from the mystery of birth to the mystery of death.

5. **RESPONSE TO 'THE SIGNS OF THE TIMES'**

There are of course many issues which face the Christian community, but two responses are given as examples, below:

— the Building of Small Christian Communities
— the Courage to Challenge the Abuse of Power.

a. Two excellent codes on **Small Christian Communities** are:

— the film 'New Day in Brazil' (Radharc)
— the slide show, 'The Journey of a People'
    from Sao Paulo Diocese.
    (See Resource Chapter for Details.)

Both of these are excellent codes for initiating a discussion.

Discussion on small Christian communities

1. What struck you particularly in the film or slide show?
2. What similiarities and what differences did you see between the situation here and that in Brazil in
    — the daily life of the people,
    — the part played by government,
    — the response of the church?
3. Do you feel we can learn anything from the church in Brazil? If so, what?

Reflection

Liberation has brought into strong focus the centrality of community in Christian revelation. We must be ready to lose our lives, to be converted, from isolation and selfishness, to community. Small Christian communities are the concrete expression of the church as a community committed to liberation. Through them renewal can take place at every level. It is there that, in openness and dialogue, people can experience the interaction of their own individual story and God's story.

In the small community each one of us is challenged to personal conversion. Each one of us is challenged to face the question, 'In what way do I dominate others?' We have to recognise that domination and dependence are not just evils 'out there', but they begin right inside ourselves. This recognition and the search for conversion makes the Christian commitment for liberation different from that in many political parties. Unless there is a change of direction in one's life, from selfishness to a life with others, we cannot be channels of liberation. This personal and group conversion is basic if the small community is to be a 'leaven'.

The church is not meant to be an institution with service stations throughout the world providing the sacraments for 'consumer Christians'. It is a communion of small Christian communities, coming together to fashion a new humanity, a better world. In the first centuries after Christ, the church converted people not by attacking them apostolically, but by the radiant witness of small groups of people really sharing and caring for one another.

The small community, in which people take an active role, works against the experience of 'massification'. Both in society and in the church, people have been made to feel helpless and then they are helpless. The church has reinforced this.

When the clergy are the only active element and the people are surrounded by Holy Fathers and Holy Mothers, then the people are kept in a state of dependence. Participation and shared responsibility become keys ideas in building small Christian communities. All share the responsibility for proclamation, communion and service (Kerygma, Koinonia, and Diakonia).

---

b. **The Courage to Challenge**

The films, 'El Salvador', 'For People or for Power', or 'These Men are Dangerous' can lead to a good discussion on the challenge to resist exploitation and oppression.

Reflection

'Happy the peacemakers:
they shall be called the children of God.
Happy those who are persecuted in the cause of right:
theirs is the kingdom of heaven.
Happy are you when people abuse you and persecute you and speak all kinds of calumny against you on my account. Rejoice and be glad, for your reward will be great in heaven." (Mt. 5:9 – 12)

"A big landowner invited me to celebrate Mass at his establishment. All his workers were there; hundreds of them. If I preach and say, for example, that one must obey one's employer, and one must work with patience and goodwill and do one's duty, for this landowner I am 'a tremendous bishop', 'a holy bishop'. But if, while speaking of the worker's duty and the landowner's rights, I have the audacity, yes, the audacity, to mention the worker's rights and the landowner's duty, then it is quite a different matter. I am labelled 'revolutionary, a progressive, pro-communist. . . .'"*

* Dom Helder Camara, Archbishop of Recife, Brazil, *The Church and Colonialism*, Denville, New Jersey: Dimension books, 1969, p. 43

---

6. ARE WE BUILDING A COMMUNITY?

It is important in the middle of a workshop to evaluate the way the group is or is not becoming a community. The following questions can help the group to become critical about the way they are developing a community.

Evaluation Questions

a. What has helped us during this week to experience ourselves as a small Christian community?

b. What has been hindering us from becoming a community so far?

c. What suggestions do we have to foster the growth of community during the rest of this workshop?

7. CO-RESPONSIBILITY

Reflection

The church is a charismatic community, not primarily a hierarchy. During the Vatican Council a few courageous bishops such as Cardinal Suenens challenged strongly the hierarchical emphasis, and the final document deals first of all, with the church as the 'Gift of the Spirit', the community of believers. The hierarchical elements are part of this, and not the other way round. There are many different gifts, given by the same Spirit. Authority is one of these, among the others, and not opposed to them. There is a specific role for the hierarchy, but always within the context of co-responsibility in the whole charismatic community.

Co-responsibility means recognition that responsibility for the life and growth of the church, for the work of the Kingdom belongs to the whole community of believers. It is intimately linked with the concern for personal and community growth. The only way for the people to grow is by taking responsibility for their own lives and for the community.

An Exercise: Role Expectations

The exercise called 'Role Expections' found in Chapter 10 can be directly applied to the church structure. It helps build a community in which all can make their most meaningful contribution.

Reflection

It is the Christian community as a whole that must respond to the needs of the whole human community in the spirit of loving compassion which Jesus showed so strikingly in his life. This involves not only responding to immediate suffering, but trying to remove the causes of man-made suffering. In the past the laity became very passive because they were so dependent on the clergy. As Nyerere said, 'The church has turned the people into a state of perpetual adolescence.' Now the laity are called again to participate actively and share responsibility fully in the response of the Christian community to the needs of its own members, and those of the whole human family.

However as the small Christian communities grow in faith and action, the role of the ordained ministers will become more, not less, clear. There is a specific role for the priest in fostering relationships at all levels. Even if in the future, people are ordained just to celebrate the Eucharist in the small communities, there will still be the need for priests and ministers at the wider parish level. There are many gifts of the Spirit for building up the community, and among these must be included that of harmonising, reconciling and fostering true communion.

Christ came as a reconciler, and that ministry has to be carried on in the church. The priest is primarily a minister of reconciliation. He presides over the Eucharist, which is specifically the sacrament of many becoming one. As the priest exercises the role of reconciler in the Eucharist, he should also be reconciling and bringing together in daily life the members of the Christian community.

8.   **God's Universal Saving Will**

Final Evaluation

The following questions are useful to evaluate our own workshop community.

a.   What has helped us during this week to experience ourselves as a small Christian community? Do temporary communities of this type have any importance in the life of the church? If so, how?

b.   What would have helped us more effectively to become a community for this time?

c.   What can we do to foster the growth of meaningful Christian communities in our own situation?

Reflection

The universal church has her own lifeline as she moves from the great biblical concept of justice towards peace, all creation in harmony.

The small Christian communities should never see themselves in isolation. The parish becomes a communion of communities, and it is important that all should have a sense of the living structure of the whole church, also in relation to the wider working of God's saving will through other churches and religions.

Vatican II has been called the conversion of the Catholic church. She is once again becoming the pilgrim church, in dialogue with others, also pilgrims, open to the Signs of the Times.

"Then I saw a new heaven and a new earth; the first heaven and the first earth had disappeared now, and there was no longer any sea. I saw the holy city, and the New Jerusalem, coming down from God out of heaven, as beautiful as a bride all dressed for her husband. Then I heard a loud voice call from the throne, 'You see this city? Here God lives among people. He will make his home among them; they shall be his people, and he will be their God; his name is God-with-them. He will wipe away all tears from their eyes; there will be no more death, and no more mourning or sadness. The world of the past has gone.'

"Then the One sitting on the throne spoke: 'Now I am making the whole of creation new.' "

Revelation 21:1 – 5

JESUS AND THE LIBERATION OF WOMEN (workshop outline)*

1. Introductions

2. Listening exercise in 4's:
    a. What do you like about being a woman?
    b. What do you dislike about being a woman?
    c. What would you like to see changed in the situation of women in the next five years?
    d. What helped and what hindered good communication during that exercise?
    e. What could we do to make sure there is good communication in this group?

3. Liberation Code (alternative version see Chapter 3).

4. The situation of women in traditional Jewish culture. Genesis 2:18 – 24, 3:16 – 20. Creation story.
    In the following stories, what do you notice about the attitude towards, and the situation of women? Small groups can study and report on different stories.
    Genesis 15:22. Abraham and Sarah
    Genesis 24. 26:14. ch. 27. Isaac and Rebecca
    Genesis 28:31. Jacob, Leah and Rachel.
    Genesis 34:36. The families of Jacob and Esau.
    Genesis 37:39. Joseph.

5. Exceptional women in the Old Testament
    The Bible was written by men and is mainly about men, but there are some stories of exceptional women. These stories can be used as codes for discussion.

Debora	Judges 4:4 – 10. 5
Ruth	Book of Ruth chapters 1 – 4.
Judith	Book of Judith 2:1 – 13, 4:8 – 15, 7 – 13, 16:21 – 30.
Esther	Book of Esther 1 – 3, 4:1 – 17, 5 – 8.
Susannah	Daniel 13.

---

* We are grateful to Bette Ekaya whose brilliant workshops on Women and the Bible in Kenya inspired and taught us much.

6.   Jesus brings a change by relating to women in a completely new way.
        Luke 8:1 – 3.   The women disciples of Jesus.
        Luke 10:38 – 47   Mary and Martha
        John 11 – 12:7
        Luke 7:36 – 50   The women at Simon's house
        John 8:3 – 11   The woman they wanted to stone
        John 4:5 – 42   The Samaritan woman at the well
        Luke 8:40 – 56   The woman with the issue of blood
                               The raising of Jairus' daughter
        John 20:11 – 18   Mary Magdalene, the first disciple to announce the
                               Resurrection

7.   Women in the early church
        Acts 16:11 – 15   Lydia
        Acts 18:1 – 4,
        18 – 21   Priscilla and Aquila
        Gal. 3:26 – 28   'No longer male nor female, but a new creation. . . .'

8.   In what ways does the church
        — raise the dignity of women?
        — restrict women from making their full contribution?

9.   What can we do to make the influence of women more effective in the
        church? In the community?

Definition of terms

Group leader is a general term including the whole range of different styles of leadership.

A facilitator sets up a process for group discussions and decision-making, and then the group identify and deal with problems in the process of their own work. As far as content and outcome are concerned, the facilitator is strictly neutral.

An animator has identified with the struggle of a particular group of people and is not necessarily neutral. Respecting the fact that transformation must come from within a group, the animator helps them to identify and achieve their own goals. To stimulate awareness, critical thinking and skill practice (s)he may introduce codes, exercises and other problem-posing techniques.

Content is the subject of a discussion — **what** the people are talking about.

Process is the way in which people are discussing — **how** the exchange between them is taking place.

A generative theme is an issue about which a group of people have such strong feelings that they cannot sit still. They want to get up and do something about the matter. The word 'generative' comes from 'to generate', to give life.

A code is a picture, story or drama which presents to the group a very familiar problem about which they have strong feelings.

The psycho-social method is another name for the Paulo Freire method of adult education. It links the feelings of individual people with the factual social context, and challenges individuals and groups to take responsibility for shaping their own lives, their environment and their community. Some people interpreted this phrase to mean a deep concern for each person, plus a recognition that it is only in the community that the individual person's needs can be fully met. A true 'psycho-socialist' was seen as one committed to 'socialism with a human face'.

The problem-posing approach is an educational method in which the attention of the group is focused on a problem of concern to all. Everybody becomes involved in a common search to understand the root causes of the problem, and to find solutions, recognising that each has a contribution to make, and that no one person has all the answers.

The non-directive method is an approach to group leadership in which the group is totally responsible for the direction taken. The Freire method is not non-directive because, though the themes are chosen by the participants, the questions used are open-ended, and the outcome of a discussion is up to the group, still the animator does challenge the group to take a series of steps; which will lead to clearer analysis and action planning.

Organisational development is the process through which an organisation, or movement, develops a strong sense of purpose and unity, mainly through clarifying its goals and establishing a good system of communication.

Multi-nationals are huge business companies, usually formed through the merging of many smaller firms, which do business in many different countries and in which the owners belong to many different nations.

Transnationals is a more recent term used to stress that while most of the so-called multi-national companies do business in many different countries, the owners may be mainly of one nationality.

Index

Bracketed figures in this index refer to chapters apportioned to the three books. Book 1 covers chapters 1 – 4, Book 2 chapters 5 – 8 and Book 3 chapters 9 – 12. The non-bracketed figures refer to page numbers which do not run on but start afresh with every book. Bracketed letter (R) refers to section *Resources* at the end of Book 1.